BETTER
THAN YOU THINK
YOU ARE

BETTER THAN YOU THINK YOU ARE

Ardeth G. Kapp

DESERET
BOOK

SALT LAKE CITY, UTAH

Library of Congress Cataloging-in-Publication Data

Kapp, Ardeth Greene, 1931–
  Better than you think you are / Ardeth G. Kapp.
      p.   cm.
  Includes bibliographical references and index.
  ISBN 1-59038-380-X (hardbound : alk. paper)
  1. Christian life—Mormon authors. 2. Self-perception—Religious life—Christianity. I. Title.
  BX8656.K36 2005
  248.4'89332—dc22   2004025651

Printed in the United States of America   72076
Publishers Printing, Salt Lake City, UT

10   9   8   7   6   5   4   3   2   1

To my beloved Heber,
who for over half a century has helped me
feel good about myself

CONTENTS

ACKNOWLEDGMENTS

The inspiration for the title of this book comes from the words of my dear friend Carolyn Rasmus, who served as the administrative assistant in the Young Women office during the eight years I served as president. For her wisdom, her humor, and her dedication, inspiration, and constant encouragement of "you're better than you think you are," I'll be forever grateful.

I express gratitude for the encouragement of Sheri Dew and Jana Erickson and for the suggestions from Cathy Chamberlain, Wendy Watson, and Kathleen Lubeck Petersen, who read the manuscript. And thanks to the editor, Jay A. Parry, and the graphic designer, Sheryl Smith, who have contributed to the final publication of this book.

INTRODUCTION

$\mathcal{D}$ear Friend,

How I wish I could chat with you, friend to friend, heart to heart, and face to face. In my mind I imagine inviting you into my home. We would sit near the fireplace side by side in comfy chairs. With the warmth of the crackling fire we would share thoughts and feelings that lift and build. It might be that we could meet in your home in your kitchen around your table, sharing a little treat as we visit. Or imagine us walking together down a path in a beautiful wooded area, or maybe at the beach, with the sound of the waves washing upon the seashore. You choose the location for our shared experience, and I'll meet you there through the following pages with stories, experiences, and insights from life that have been important and helpful to me over the years.

It is my sincere desire that these insights and stories will be helpful to you and that the Spirit of the Lord will carry the idea of each message deep into your heart, so that in times of discouragement, when you need a lift, you will remember that you are *better than you think you are!* It is not always easy to acknowledge, but the truth remains: in many ways, you are.

With love,

Your sister

I will go before your face. I will be on your right hand
and on your left, and my Spirit shall be in your hearts,
and mine angels round about you, to bear you up.

—Doctrine and Covenants 84:88

WE ARE NOT ALONE

There is great power that emanates from good
women who, in the midst of the pressures of
the day, arise above their challenges in a
mighty force for righteousness.

I remember standing at the kitchen window of our
home, looking down the gravel road as far as I could see
across the flat Canadian prairie that led to who knows
where. My sixth-grade report card was in my hand and
tears were in my eyes. My mom was trying to comfort me:
"Just because your report card says you've failed a grade and
will be required to take the sixth grade over, that doesn't
mean *you're* a failure."

"But, Mom," I insisted in anguish, holding up the evidence to prove my failure. Not only was I horrified about
what my friends might think, but I *felt* like a failure.

My mother came to my rescue as only a mother can:

"You forget you were at a disadvantage because of the classes you missed when you were sick."

Then my father spoke up. He had a plan, he said, a plan he assured me would work and have me ready for the seventh grade when school started in the fall. The plan would work if I was willing to do my part. "Through the summer months," he explained, "we'll work together on your arithmetic and spelling. If you try your very best, I promise you will be ready for the seventh grade on time."

I had great faith in my father and his plan, even though I had little faith in my own ability at that stressful time.

With my father's almost daily tutoring and my mom's encouragement and confidence, by midsummer I passed the required tests and qualified for the next grade. With my father and mother's help, I began to realize, I could do far better than I ever thought possible, in many things. They knew me. They knew things about me that I had not yet discovered. I was their offspring and had inherited qualities from them and divine qualities from our Heavenly Father. Well, maybe I had not inherited an aptitude in arithmetic and spelling, but I had inherited what I needed for all the courses that really matter.

I knew then that the tests would continue, and they have. They are an essential part of our mortal experience.

JUST ONE STEP AT A TIME

If we consider the possibility of trying to advance from grade to grade in our lives without our Father's help, we will always feel inadequate. There have been times in my life when I have experienced discouragement. I have prayed about unfulfilled expectations and the purpose of my life. When we ponder our lives, we all realize that we are less now than we have the capacity to become.

Yet when we accept our Father's invitation to be tutored by him through the gift of the Holy Ghost, we are far better than we think we are. We can be lifted and strengthened and magnified by the power of the Spirit, which is available to each of us as we face the tests in life. We are promised, "Yea, behold, I will tell you in your mind and in your heart, by the Holy Ghost, which shall come upon you and which shall dwell in your heart" (D&C 8:2).

These feelings of being less than we want to be or should be are not restricted to childhood. In fact, the feeling seems to increase as we study the doctrine that gives us ultimate direction: "Be ye therefore perfect, even as your Father which is in heaven is perfect" (Matthew 5:48).

This admonition to become perfect is not to discourage us, but actually to give us encouragement. It gives us reason to believe that it is our destiny to be like our Father—a destiny that is not only desirable but possible because of

3

the plan our Father has for us. It is to be accomplished one step at a time, not always according to our own schedule, but "line upon line, precept upon precept; and I will try you and prove you herewith," he tells us (D&C 98:12). It is our opportunity to come to know not only who we are, but *whose* we are, and to feel glad.

RIGHTEOUS SELF-RESPECT

Even as we are striving for a destination that is a long distance away, an understanding of our possibilities as we follow our Father's plan gives hope, faith, promise, and yes, anticipation. I have learned that an eternal perspective helps ease our sense of urgency as we strive with a natural desire to be better than we are. Could we, should we ever demean ourselves and lose confidence when we consider the price the Savior has paid in our behalf and when we know we are the offspring of God? "And if children, then heirs; heirs of God, and joint-heirs with Christ; if so be that we suffer with him, that we may be also glorified together" (Romans 8:17).

Consider the prayer of the Old English weaver, quoted by President Harold B. Lee: "Oh God, help me to hold a high opinion of myself." He goes on to say, "That should be the prayer of every soul. Not an abnormally developed self-esteem that becomes haughtiness, conceit, or arrogance. But a righteous self respect that might be defined as belief in one's own worth, worth to God and worth to man."[1]

And our beloved prophet, President Gordon B. Hinckley, gives us this encouragement and direction: "When a man is motivated by great and powerful convictions of truth, then he disciplines himself . . . because of the knowledge within his heart that God lives, that he is a child of God with an eternal and limitless potential."[2]

When we deny or discredit our own possibilities, our divine nature, or our individual worth, we discredit our Creator. The Lord does not want us to become discouraged when for one reason or another we feel we have failed. He doesn't want us to spend all our lives in the sixth grade. With his plan and with his help, we can be prepared for the next grade and the next and the next. We will be on time when that next class begins. And should we feel the devastation of failing a grade, I have learned that he will be there to help us again and again.

One Heart and One Mind

Far too often, good women striving to keep up with the demands of worthy goals feel the burden of discouragement. They may feel the pressure that comes with wondering if they are keeping up. We must not give way to the constant, subtle, but destructive influence of the adversary, who seeks to have good women demean themselves and others and cause them to focus on what may appear to be failure. When Latter-day Saint women become united in lifting and building themselves and those around them, avoiding comparing and competing, they create a power that is very threatening to the cause of Satan. Such unity is a powerful weapon against his plan.

The war that began in heaven is still raging. We were the valiant and faithful then, and we must be now. Because of our commitment then and now, we sometimes feel the need to drive ourselves beyond the breaking point, resulting in feelings of exhaustion and of being overwhelmed. These feelings are not unfamiliar in today's world. It is one of the enemy's tactics to weaken the mighty influence of righteous women, who are in the midst of what sometimes seem insurmountable challenges. The enemy seeks to instill feelings of failure in us, as well as a false sense of being unloved, unappreciated, and unworthy.

Make no mistake: these feelings, even if justified at times, must not be nurtured and fed. The cost is too high. It will take the joy out of living. Let us never forget the encouraging words of President James E. Faust: "When ... sin, disappointment, failure, and weakness make us less than we should ever be, there can come the healing salve of the unreserved love in the grace of God. It is a love . . . that lifts and blesses. It is a love that sustains a new beginning."[3]

In my life I have felt the love of our Savior, as I'm sure you have. That love he has for each one of us "sustains a new beginning," a renewed determination when we go through challenging times. Challenges provide opportunities to learn and grow and to gain a new perspective and be rejuvenated with feelings of joy and happiness. As one of our young missionaries, after a season of learning, expressed in his weekly letter to the mission president, "Dear President, this diligence and obedience stuff you have been talking about is finally beginning to kick in." He had gained a new perspective from his struggle. He felt the love of God and was eager to respond to God's call to higher service. He began to realize his potential more fully. He became a great missionary.

It is a fact that we have been called to take our place on the stage of life at a historic time in the history of the Church and the world. The Lord is counting on us. There is great power that emanates from good women who rise above discouragement and despair and with faith and trust reach out to others in unity. A number of years ago I was assigned to go to Washington, D.C., to participate in a national leadership task force. The diversity among this group of good women was impressive—ranging from culture, age, and faith, to language—yet all were united in a cause to help protect the family and society. After an opening prayer, one of the women rose from her seat to make this significant, brief observation, which was felt by everyone present. "One woman," she said, "is helpful; ten women are influential; one hundred are powerful; one thousand are invincible." Why was that true? Because we were *united*.

"And the Lord called his people Zion, because they were of one heart and one mind, and dwelt in righteousness; and there was no poor among them" (Moses 7:18). I believe those among us who are suffering from attacks of self-depreciation are among the most poor. It is a spiritual hunger more severe than physical hunger. When we join in unity, with "one heart and one mind," good women can feed those—including themselves—who hunger at times for a feeling of acceptance.

Ammon testified that in God's strength "I can do all things"; and in his strength "many mighty miracles we have wrought in this land, for which we will praise his name forever" (Alma 26:11).

We are not alone! As we stand in unity with one another, and as we truly seek to work with the strength of the Lord, remembering that we are his children and that he has a plan for us, we will see "many mighty miracles" in our sphere of influence at this historic time when the Lord is counting on us.

What is man, that thou art mindful of him? and the son of man,
that thou visitest him? For thou hast made him a little lower than the
angels, and hast crowned him with glory and honour.

—PSALM 8:4–5

2

BETTER THAN YOU THINK YOU ARE

WE ARE NOT GOOD JUDGES OF OURSELVES AS WE
REACH FOR GOALS THAT MAY BELONG TO ANOTHER
SEASON OF OUR LIVES.

id I do okay?" Most of us, maybe all of us, ask
that at one time or another. We want to feel that our
efforts have been acceptable and that we have not let
anyone down. A word of sincere commendation is like
a ray of sunshine that brings a smile to the face and a
warm feeling to the heart. While serving as the Young
Women General President of the Church, I felt the
need and desire on many occasions to be more capable
in relation to the responsibilities I had been given.
There were times when the enemy of thought would
arouse in my mind an awareness of my inadequacies

and imperfections. Often those feelings would creep in like tiny termites to weaken my confidence just as I was on my way to make a presentation to the Brethren.

At such times, even though I may not have mentioned my concern, my dear friend Carolyn Rasmus (who served as the administrative assistant in the Young Women office and who played a major role in the work that was being done at that time), would know just what to do. In a very quiet voice, almost like a whisper, she would say, "You are better than you think you are."

Her words would always make me smile. They were a most welcome reminder. I knew that if I were functioning on my own I would have a legitimate reason to feel inadequate, but when I did my best to prepare and then trusted in the Lord, he would magnify me far beyond my natural ability. This happened many times.

Some years later, while serving with my husband in the Canada Vancouver Mission, I would see young men and women come into the mission field with a desire to do their very best. But they often didn't reach the sometimes unrealistic goals they set for themselves, and they would become discouraged. Some would begin to lose confidence. It was easy for me to identify those who, feeling the weight of the responsibility they had been given, wondered if they could measure up.

On such occasions, I would remember the encouraging words of my dear friend Carolyn. I would then stand or sit by that missionary and quietly and sincerely say, "You are better than you think you are." When they heard that, their countenance would immediately change from frown to smile. It was a testimony to observe the magnificence of these young men and women and their increasing ability as they turned to the Lord and kept going.

After I heard these struggling but wonderful missionaries give presentations in zone conference, I would often write them a brief note, commenting on specific positive things I noticed. The note frequently included a little rating, on a scale of one to ten, of something they could improve in—perhaps relating to the need for a haircut or an ironed shirt or polished shoes. But always the note included the reminder, "You are better than you think you are."

After I had been doing this for some time, I thought I should ask one of our very mature APs (assistants to the president) if he thought my notes were a good idea—or did "guys" think it was a bit of nonsense? Without hesitation he opened his jacket. There, in the inside pocket, were several notes. He said, "I have kept every note you have given me."

I continued the practice of writing and delivering these brief notes, especially to those who seemed to be lacking in confidence. But then I learned that even those who appeared confident appreciated a note. We all face responsibilities that seem overwhelming at times. We all have recurring feelings of falling short of our desire to do better. And we all have ample evidence that we are far from perfect. We can take comfort in the statement of Elder Neal A. Maxwell: "The first thing to be said of this feeling of inadequacy is that it is normal."[1] When you feel that you are doing your best and it is not good enough, a little note or whisper from someone you trust helps lift the load. Would you not keep such a note? Of course you would.

Several years after our mission I was speaking at a young adult conference in Arizona. I was very pleased to see three of our beloved elders in attendance. I did not have an opportunity to speak to them prior to the meeting, but afterward they waited until others had left and then stepped forward with big smiles and handed me a note. I knew immediately that the tables had been turned, and I was the one being evaluated.

I read the note while they stood watching for my response. They had made many positive comments about my message, just as I had earlier done for them. Then they included a rating on my missionary attire. On a scale of one to ten, I received an eight. "Just a little bright for a missionary," was the comment, which I took as a compliment. With such support, I felt in that moment that the content of my message and delivery had been better than I thought it was. I kept their note.

The other day I received a letter in the mail. It read in part, "Ardeth, this is an excellent report! Congratulations. You are better than in 1997. Superb! You are better than most women . . . of your age. Excellent." Actually it was a report from my doctor regarding a bone density test I had taken, but even on bones it's good to get an encouraging message! I kept that note too.

NOTES OF ENCOURAGEMENT

Notes of encouragement, even to strangers, can have a lasting impact on the sender as well as the receiver. On October 11, 1986, the date of the first Young Women Worldwide Celebration, young women throughout the world united in the power of righteousness. On that historic morning, young women wrote brief messages of love, hope, and testimony and attached them to helium-filled balloons. At a given hour their messages were released and carried by the winds far and wide.

Notes attached to the helium-filled balloons were released in Ireland, Turkey, New Zealand, Bolivia, and in many other areas of the world. One sample of the thousands of messages that were sent on that historic day:

> I am 15 years old and a member of The Church of Jesus Christ of Latter-day Saints. I know that God lives and loves us. Jesus Christ is the Savior of the world. I love him with all my heart. If I could wish for anything for the world, I would wish that everyone had a sure knowledge that God lives and that he hears and answers prayers. I'm thankful for the answers I've received to my prayers. You too can receive answers to your prayers. All you have to do is ask. No matter who you are or what you have done, God will listen.
>
> Rosanna, Anchorage, Alaska

And two days after Tatia, a Laurel from Richmond

Branch in Australia, sent her message aloft, she received this reply:

> I found your balloon in Emu Plains, NSW. I think your message is beautiful and nothing is impossible. They are the things I want too. I will treasure your letter forever.
>
> Sarah

One young woman who released her balloon in Fordyce, Arkansas, received the following response from a man who lives in Kentucky:

> Hi, Mary Smith. My name is David, and I live on a farm around Hopkinsville, Kentucky. Guess what? I found your note while cutting hay in the field on my daddy's farm. Almost mowed it over until I noticed that there was a note on the package, so I decided to get off my tractor and look at it. Then I saw it was a note, so I killed my tractor and took the time to see what it had to say. That was the first time I ever found something like this, and it really gave me a good feeling inside knowing there were still good people left in the world today.

Following this eventful day, when helium balloons filled the skies carrying messages of love, encouragement, and testimony throughout the world, one of the

General Authorities said to me, "We have always known about the sons of Helaman and their fight for righteousness. Now we know about the daughters of Helium."

"BE OF GOOD CHEER"

When we feel the need for encouragement, when we wonder and sometimes worry about our worth, when we feel impatient concerning our progress toward perfection, the Lord sends us "notes" for us to read—he sends a whispering in our ear that speaks to our heart and mind, a whispering we can hear when we listen with the Spirit.

Listen to Christ's gentle words of tender understanding as he refers to us as little children: "Verily, verily, I say unto you, ye are little children, and ye have not as yet understood how great blessings the Father hath in his own hands and prepared for you; and ye cannot bear all things now; nevertheless, be of good cheer, for I will lead you along. The kingdom is yours and the blessings thereof are yours, and the riches of eternity are yours" (D&C 78:17–18).

Remember, God is our Father and we are his children. Knowing that he will lead us along from day to day gives us reason to be cheerful. When our weaknesses, our mortality, press upon us and we catch ourselves comparing and competing to do better than someone else, we lose sight of God's plan and forget our true identity. Our weakness, our mortality, is designed to have a more positive purpose: to help us be humble and willing to turn to the Lord. As we do, he "will make weak things become strong" (Ether 12:27). It is reassuring to know that we are not alone in our struggle to overcome our weaknesses and do better.

Even prophets deal with feelings of weakness. The Book of Mormon gives a helpful example of a prophet who deeply felt his own inadequacy. Nephi wrote that he would fulfill his responsibility to make a record "notwithstanding my weakness" (2 Nephi 33:11).

Too often we measure our daily performance against the admonition to one day become "perfect even as . . . your Father who is in Heaven is perfect" (3 Nephi 12:48). Lest we become discouraged, it is important to understand and remember the process by which we grow spiritually. It is not intended that we should reach perfection in this life. On one occasion Joseph Smith said, "When you climb up a ladder, you must begin at the bottom and ascend step by step until you arrive at the top; and so it is with the principles of the gospel—you must begin with the first, and go on until you have learned all of the principles of exaltation. But it will be a great while after you have passed through the veil before you will have learned them. It is not all to be comprehended in this world; it will be a great work to learn our salvation and exaltation even beyond the grave."[2]

We are not good judges of ourselves as we reach for goals that may actually belong to another season of our lives. We must learn patience as we grow line upon line and do all that is expected of us at a given time, knowing that we are not required to become perfect in this life.

The Lord knows us, knows our potential, and knows the desires of our hearts. On those days when you feel like you are falling behind, even after you have given it all you've got, carry in your heart and your mind this note from him who understands: "And see that all . . . things are done in wisdom and order; for it is not requisite that a man should run faster than he has strength" (Mosiah 4:27).

President Joseph F. Smith taught these comforting words: "God does not judge men as we do, nor look upon them in the same light we do. He knows our imperfections, all the causes, the 'whys and wherefores' are made manifest unto him. He judges us by our acts and the intents of our hearts. His judgments will be true, just, and righteous. Ours are obscured by the imperfections of man."³

When you question whether you are as good as you ought to be or want to be, be happy with the progress you *have* made—even at those times when you may have missed reading your scriptures, raised your voice in frustration, lost patience while waiting in line at the grocery store, failed to have the house tidy, or gotten upset with your husband over some misunderstanding.

I know that last feeling. Heber and I had been in the mission field only a few weeks. We were both committed to do the very best we could. So then why were we having these disagreements? Why did I feel so frustrated at times? He had previously served as a stake president, and I had just been released as the Young Women General President. I thought everything would be smooth sailing.

While traveling in the car, which gave us no choice but to stay close, I considered one of my frustrations. It had to do with the policy of how mission office staff were to answer the telephone. One person had the responsibility to answer the phone, with a backup assigned if the first was unavailable. Heber had directed that the telephone was to ring several times before the second in line was to pick it up. Years before, I had worked as a training instructor for the telephone company, and I had been programmed to pick the phone up on the first ring, even in the middle of the night. I felt very confident about the value of such a policy. That approach continued to be a priority during the time I was in the Young Women office. In fact, I emphasized it enough that on one occasion when I was leaving for an overseas assignment and several of the secretaries in the YW office came to see me off, they teasingly carried a large sign that read, "Don't worry, the phones are covered"—and in small letters at the bottom—"with a towel."

Without mentioning my frustrations about this particular matter, I voiced my thoughts as we drove along. "We have both had years of experience being president. Why am I feeling frustrated?" Heber, with a big smile, looked straight ahead at the highway that would lead us to our zone conference. After pausing, perhaps waiting for me to make the discovery, he simply said, "Maybe that is part of the problem. We only need one president."

The reality of that valuable insight changed my perspective and our relationship on such matters. I realized that my concern for how and when the phone was to be answered might have interfered with the spirit of unity that is essential when we are about the Lord's work, especially in our families. Life is filled with interesting discoveries about ourselves all along the path, including some things we like and some things we want to change.

The Savior tells us to "be of good cheer" (John 16:33), and gives these comforting words: "Behold, ye are little children and ye cannot bear all things now; ye must grow in grace and in the knowledge of the truth" (D&C 50:40). He is the one who will judge us because he knows us; he knows the "whys and wherefores" and the intents of our hearts.

GOOD FRUIT RIPENS AT DIFFERENT SEASONS

However, we must not delay our progress. President Hinckley gives us this counsel: "I have been quoted as saying 'Do the best you can.' But I want to emphasize that it be the very best. We are too prone to be satisfied with mediocre performance. We are capable of doing so much better."[4]

In my role as a mission president's wife, I was mindful of one young man who was having a struggle adapting, adjusting, and making a major change in his lifestyle. He showed up at a zone conference wearing roller blades and a ball cap. It appeared that he was not reaching for the next rung on the ladder. That evening at supper my husband and I were discussing the need to help this young man make the transition and come to realize his potential. After some discussion President Kapp said, "Well, we'll just send 'em home."

I sat up straight, my eyes wide open with all the nurturing instinct of a mission mom, and I spoke with alarm. "Send *him* home? For wearing roller blades?"

Heber smiled, settled my concern, and said, "No, send the roller blades home."

Everyone grows on a mission. As all good fruit ripens at different seasons, so do good missionaries. We must remember that we did not come to this earth to gain our worth—we brought it with us. We were the valiant and faithful ones who kept our first estate, who chose to come to earth and follow the Lord's plan, knowing that with his help we could keep our second estate (see Abraham 3:26) and reach our ultimate goal in spite of the struggles along the way—or maybe because of the struggles. President George Q. Cannon reminds us: "Now you are in your second estate and you are going to be tested again. The men and women that will be loyal under these circumstances God will exalt, because it will be the highest test to which they can be subjected."[5]

Let us make every effort and pray earnestly as we fight against thoughts that will loom up wearing different masks, seeking to catch us off guard and creep in like termites to put in question our worth.

How Much Are You Worth?

There are wonderful notes in the scriptures that can carry the words of the Savior into our minds and hearts. They lift our spirits and help us realize that with the Lord's help we can always do far, far better than we can by ourselves.

In our society today we have a way of determining an item's worth by the monetary price we place on things. For example, consider the enormous cost of scientific exploration or medical research—and how we value the practical results of such work. Consider what you would be willing to pay for a glass of cold water if you were thirsting to death. This practice of putting a price on things serves to underscore their worth.

When we consider our own individual worth (see D&C 18:10), we must remember that we have been bought with a price, a price that only Christ can redeem (see 1 Corinthians 7:23). As we come to an awareness of his unconditional love for us and the enormous and incomprehensible price paid in our behalf, we begin to more fully sense our worth, even in our imperfect state. He tells us, "I have graven thee upon the palms of my hands" (Isaiah 49:16).

The scriptures are notes from God to teach us about the incomprehensible and far-reaching blessings of the atonement. It is in turning to the Savior and placing our trust in his redeeming love that we can realize our true worth and the price he paid in our behalf.

> *I think of his hands pierced and bleeding to pay*
> *   the debt!*
> *Such mercy, such love, and devotion can I*
> *   forget?*
> *No, no, I will praise and adore at the mercy*
> *   seat,*
> *Until at the glorified throne I kneel at his feet.*
> *Oh, it is wonderful that he should care for me*
> *Enough to die for me!*[6]

THE GOOD YOU ARE AND THE GOOD YOU DO

As we learn about our Lord and Savior through the scriptures and through the Holy Ghost, we also learn about *ourselves*. Sometimes it's far too easy to forget who we really are in an eternal sense. The Lord sends us precious notes to teach us the things we need to know to value ourselves as God values us.

As good women face the enormous, demanding, constant, ever-present, and sacred challenges of motherhood, especially in today's world, there will always be many things left undone, overlooked, and ignored. It is all too easy to let the challenges of life overpower our ability to acknowledge the good we are and the good we do.

My dear mother, like many (maybe most) mothers, was much, much better than she ever thought she was. She would frequently remind herself (especially on Mother's Day) about all the things she didn't do that she thought good mothers always do. But she failed to tally—and in some cases she wasn't even aware of— the very significant gifts she was passing on to her children just by her honest, dedicated determination to rally to the mission of motherhood in her own inspiring way. Cooking and sewing were not her thing, and she didn't teach me and my two sisters, Sharon and Shirley, what might be considered the art of homemaking. But she was a master in the attributes of selfless sacrifice, love, service, and providing a vision of possibilities and creative ways to achieve worthwhile goals and give us wings. She was tireless in her dedication to her family as she took care of our small country store next to our home, where we learned at an early age to respect the goodness of all people—the Hutterites (a religious group from the nearby colonies who dressed differently), the Indians from across the river, and everyone else who came through the doors of our little establishment.

Our mother was one who did all that and more. She did a great multitude of things that were accomplished in a near-miraculous way but that are left unrecorded except in the heart and soul of her children, "written not with ink, but with the Spirit of the living God; not in tables of stone, but in fleshy tables of the heart" (2 Corinthians 3:3).

The recognition and admiration of others is not the standard to which we aspire. We must not measure our worth as a mother or wife or neighbor except by the standards the Lord has set. And we must remember that only he truly understands the individual gifts, the talents, and the heart and intent of every mother and every child of God, who must find his or her own way in life, guided by the Spirit and in harmony with gospel principles.

A fable tells of a group of animals who organized a school. In order to make it easier to administer the curriculum and evaluate progress, the animals decided that every animal student was to take the same subjects. According to the fable, the rabbit started at the top of the class in running but had a nervous breakdown because of makeup work in swimming. The eagle was a problem child and was disciplined severely. In the climbing class he beat others to the top of the tree—but he insisted on using his own way to get there. The prairie dog stayed out of school because the administration would not add digging and burrowing to the curriculum. The very skills that made each one great individually were overlooked through a curriculum that was designed for blanket application to everyone. Yet, even though these animals may have suffered a complete sense of failure, all of them were fully capable in terms of the specific gifts that had been given to them to magnify.

The Psalmist wrote, "What is man, that thou art mindful of him? and the son of man, that thou visitest him? For thou hast made him a little lower than the angels, and hast crowned him with glory and honour" (Psalm 8:4–5).

The Lord is mindful of us, and he regards us as

beings who have been "crowned . . . with glory and honour."

Do you acknowledge the glory and honor of God's creations—including yourself? Are you ever guilty of degrading yourself? If this is ever the case, consider these inspiring words to the song "I Am of Infinite Worth," written by Joy Saunders Lundberg:

> *All I need do is remember*
> *If ever I wonder if I am of worth,*
> *Remember my Savior, what He did for me*
> *When He lived among men on the earth.*
> *Pain and unspeakable sorrow*
> *He bore for my sins there in Gethsemane.*
> *Then He gave up His life as He hung on*
>   *the cross,*
> *And He did it all for me.*
>
> *For I am of worth, of infinite worth.*
> *My Savior, Redeemer loves me.*
> *Yes, I am of worth, of infinite worth,*
> *I'll be all He wants me to be.*
> *I will praise Him, I will serve Him,*
> *I will grow in His love*
> *And fulfill my divine destiny.*

Lovingly Jesus is watching
He knows I am worth all He suffered for
* me.*
Now I must fulfill my own mission in life,
Ever following Him faithfully.
Line upon line I am striving
Not seeking the honor or praise of mankind.
I will reach for the joy of Celestial rewards,
'Til all that God offers is mine.[7]

Elder Maxwell makes this telling observation: "Some of us who would not chastise a neighbor for his frailties have a field day with our own. Some of us stand before no more harsh a judge than ourselves. A constructive critic truly cares for that which he criticizes, including himself. Whereas self pity is the most condescending form of pity, it soon cannibalizes all other concerns."[8]

There may be times when mistakes and wrong choices rob you of hope and faith. Consider this note by Elder Richard G. Scott: "God is not a jealous being who delights in persecuting those who misstep. He is an absolutely perfect, compassionate, understanding, patient, and forgiving father. He is willing to entreat, counsel, strengthen, lift and fortify."[9]

As we continue our climb up the ladder, step by

step, let us never forget who we were—the valiant and faithful. Let us remember who we are—the covenant sons and daughters of God. Let us acknowledge who we are to become with our divine inheritance. Brigham Young powerfully explained our past, present, and future: "There is no spirit but what was pure and holy when it came here from the celestial world. . . . He is the father of our spirits; and if we could know, understand, and do his will, every soul would be prepared to return back into his presence and when they get there they will see that they had formerly lived there for ages, that they had previously been acquainted with every nook and corner, with the palaces, walks and gardens; and they would embrace their father, and he would embrace them and say, 'My son, my daughter, I have you home again.' And the child would say, 'Oh my father, my father, I am here again.'"[10]

Look unto me in every thought; doubt not, fear not. . . .
Be faithful, keep my commandments, and ye
shall inherit the kingdom of heaven.

—Doctrine and Covenants 6:36–37

3

DOUBT NOT,
FEAR NOT

If we are to win in this daily battle against
the enemy, there are some crucial, precious
eternal truths we must have as much a part of
our being as the air we breathe.

It is a fact that we all have some doubts and fears. These may change according to the season we are in and the challenges and responsibilities and expectations we face, but they are very real nonetheless.

Even the very young experience these challenges. When my niece Shelly was about six years old, she and I were planning to drive by ourselves to British Columbia so I could assist my sister, who was giving birth to the eighth of her eleven children. About one hundred miles into this journey, Shelly became very concerned;

in fact, she was heartbroken. In her excitement to leave, she had forgotten Mindy and Teddy, the two dolls she slept with, played with, and loved. She had doubts and fears about the possibility of having a good time without her dolls. She was so distraught I seriously considered turning back to get them. After trying to console her with the promise that we could play her Winnie the Pooh tape all the way for two days if she wanted, I determined to continue on.

Within a few hours after arrival at our destination, Shelly was welcomed into the world of the big girls, her cousins, ages eight, ten, and upward. By the close of the second day her doubts and fears had taken a dramatic turn. The thought of Mindy and Teddy had vanished completely, at least for the time being. But then new doubts and fears entered in. I overheard a conversation in the bedroom as Jen, the older and wiser cousin, consoled Shelly on another matter. They had a tape measure and were measuring their waists. It was discovered that Shelly's waist was two inches bigger than Jen's. This gave Shelly concern until I heard Jen explain with all her eight-year-old wisdom and compassion, "Don't worry, Shelly. When you get big, your waist goes to your bust and then you will be pretty."

It seems that the enemy attacks us on every front and at every age. The doubts and fears change according to our circumstances. But they are always lurking in the shadows, waiting for any chance to invade our peace of mind, our confidence, our feelings of worth, and our glorious possibilities. The attack may be obvious, but it is usually subtle; either way, it is very real, it catches us off guard, and it throws us off balance.

As Latter-day Saint women we always want to measure up, whether it is around the waist, around the block, or with the person next door. We especially want our children to toe the mark. As Sister Pat Holland explained, "We want our children to have straight A's, straight teeth, and be straight arrows."[1] We must look good, act good, and at least give the impression of doing everything right, right?

I recall one morning about 10 o'clock. I was standing in our kitchen feeling satisfied with my day thus far, convinced that I had been doing everything I should be doing. Suddenly I heard a knock on the kitchen window. I looked up and saw my husband, who stood there with a big cardboard sign that read "Will work for food." Oh no, I thought. No breakfast and it was 10 o'clock. I wasn't doing so well after all. To my feeling of failure was added a greater concern: my neighbors (who surely were all perfect wives) might see the sign. Heber was smiling, so I just opened the door and said, "Come on in! Oh, and while you are fixing some breakfast, fix some for me too."

I made a choice. Breakfast on time is nice, but it is not one of the essentials. I decided I wasn't going to get down on myself about it—no doubt, no fear.

HOW TO MAKE YOURSELF MISERABLE

When we began our journey in this mortal life we became separated from the physical presence of our Father in Heaven. The veil was drawn, and we are now required to walk by faith. Yet from the scriptures, like letters from home, the Lord comforts us with these reassuring words: "Look unto me in every thought; doubt not, fear not" (D&C 6:36).

Sisters, if we are to handle our worries, our disappointments, our sorrows, and our tests—which are very real—we cannot, we must not succumb to measuring our worth, our success, and our approval by the standards of the world or our neighbors next door, even if they are our friends. Furthermore, we must not measure our Father in Heaven's love for us according to our performance or the way some of our most fervent prayers seem unanswered or delayed or by the mistakes we make or even by some of the dumb things we do.

I have a book on my shelf at home titled *How to Make Yourself Miserable.*[2] I get it out occasionally to see how I am doing. It gives detailed instructions about how to change worries into deeper anxieties and identifies optimum brooding times. It provides instruction on how to make yourself miserable about the past ("if only"), the present ("how come"), and even the future ("what if"). I've tried most of the suggestions on how to make myself miserable and sure enough, they work.

Sometimes it may take years to bring closure to an annoying reminder of what seemed like a major failure. When I was about fourteen years old, living in the small town of Glenwood (with a population of about 250), Alberta, our band was invited to march in the parade as part of the famous Calgary Stampede celebration. It was such an honor that the whole town was in awe, and we increased our practice time to get ready. My cousin Colleen and I and three of our friends were the drum majorettes. Colleen's mother made stunning outfits, red and white with gold epaulets, for us to wear with our boots and high silk hats. We practiced until we could twirl our batons in rhythm, throw them in the air, and catch them almost every time.

The eventful day arrived. But our performance was not what we had planned. Somehow, in this large city, Colleen and I lost our way, and the parade started without us. When we finally caught up we did our best, but I felt humiliated, to say the least.

Some sixty years would pass before I could finally bring closure to that deeply disappointing experience from my childhood. This time I was back in the great city of Calgary, not in a parade but on stage. I was one of several people who were participating in an all-day women's gathering known as Time Out for Women, sponsored by Deseret Book Company. There were approximately 1,500 women in the audience, including many friends and some relatives. The night before, as I was in the hotel room anxiously anticipating my speaking responsibilities the next day, that old memory of my performance in Calgary years before returned to my mind. The thought occurred to me that this was my chance to set things right. I called the concierge at the front desk and asked if they could get me a round wooden dowel about three feet long. In a short time, a man from the engineer's department came with a round wooden stick, obviously a "plumber's helper" with the rubber end removed. I thanked him, then quit worrying about my talk and began practicing my baton twirling. The skills all came back.

The next day when it was time for my presentation, I began by inquiring of the vast audience if any of them had locked in their mind a time when they felt like they hadn't measured up and would like to close that door forever. The response from the audience gave me courage. I related my former experience in Calgary and my sense of failure. "Now," I said, "in front of this wonderful, compassionate, nonjudgmental audience with so many friends, I would like another chance. Is that okay?" I reached down and picked up my substitute baton, which I had hidden behind the podium, and began to twirl. I twirled first with one hand and then with the other. The audience began to clap. As I continued to twirl my baton, hand over hand and around the back (including a toss in the air that never really left my hand), the audience continued clapping and started to laugh. This increased my desire to do my best. I stepped aside from the podium and added marching steps to my twirling, though not so high as in years past. At this point I received a standing ovation, with laughter and cheers even before I began my talk.

Sometimes it may take awhile to set things right

when we feel like we haven't measured up, but in areas that really matter we can set things right much more quickly. My message that day was entitled "Doubt Not, Fear Not—You Are Better Than You Think You Are."

WINNING THE BATTLE

If we are to win in this daily battle against the enemy, there are some crucial, precious, eternal truths we must have as part of our being, as much as the air we breathe. One such is the first Article of Faith, which is at the very foundation of our faith: "We believe in God, the Eternal Father, and in His Son, Jesus Christ, and in the Holy Ghost." This statement has greater meaning for me when I replace "We believe" with "I believe": "I believe in God, the Eternal Father . . ."

There are other such statements that help to strengthen me. At those times when pride creeps in through the cracks of my armor, seeking to distract me by worldly values, I repeat in my mind a variation of the first Young Women Value. It tells of our identity, our relationship with our Father in Heaven, and the eternal plan. It has great power—it helps to clear my vision and gives an eternal perspective. "I am a daughter of a Heavenly Father, who loves me, and I will have faith in His eternal plan, which centers in Jesus Christ, my Savior." That is a little sermon I have ready for recall whenever I feel negative thoughts intruding on my mind. It is a statement of our identity. It confirms our Father's eternal love for each of us individually. It states the need for our faith in the eternal plan and underscores that it all centers in our Savior and Redeemer, Jesus Christ.

It is Christ's love for us that we draw on, so we never consider giving in, giving up, or giving out. This assurance of his great love for you and for me, even as we are at this very moment, can remove the cloudy dark days that creep into our lives as part of our mortal experience. This love can remove both doubt and fear. With that love in our hearts, we can know who we are and whose we are—literally daughters and sons of God. Oh yes, we all have days when we feel like a nobody. We feel that we aren't what we should be or want to be, and we have evidence to prove it. Sometimes we carefully accumulate evidence that we are not measuring up to the Joneses, or anything else for that matter.

When we come to those days, we can remember our Father's love. Some years ago I found this statement written by President George Q. Cannon, which speaks to my heart and has sustained me. He explains our relationship with our Father in Heaven: "We're the children of God and as his children there is no attribute we ascribe to him that we do not possess, though they may be dormant or in embryo. Now this is the truth, we humble people, we who feel sometimes so worthless, so good for nothing, we are not so worthless as we think. There is not one of us but what God's love has been expended upon. There is not one of us that He has [not] cared for and caressed. We may be insignificant and contemptible in our own eyes and in the eyes of others, but the truth remains that we are the children of God and He has actually given His angels—invisible beings of power and might—charge concerning us, and they watch over us and have us in their keeping."[3]

We truly are better than we think we are. Can we question our individual worth or our divine nature or our true identity? No. Do we need reminders? Yes, we do. And each Sunday when we partake of the sacred emblems of the sacrament, we do it in remembrance of our covenants with our Father in Heaven, as we take upon us the name of his Son and commit to always remember him and keep his commandments, with the promise we will always have his Spirit to be with us when we do our part (see D&C 20:77).

Children can teach us these truths; in fact, some of our greatest lessons come from children, simple and yet so profound. On Christmas Eve our family had the tradition that we would each open one gift before retiring. One year we gathered together; the Christmas lights on the tree cast a glow over all the gifts arranged at the base of the tree. Little Shelly eagerly chose which present I was to open. Then she helped me tear the wrappings off to reveal this important gift. There it was, a beautiful orange and brown hot pad she had made herself. She was eager to see if I liked it. Of course I did. With the hot pad was a note, printed in her own careful handwriting: "Because you are so special." With one arm around her and the beautiful homemade orange-and-brown hot pad in the other hand, I said: "Oh Shelly, not *that* special."

She pulled away from me and faced me front on, as if she had taken the position of a great evangelist at the podium, and expounded this great eternal truth: "Now Mommy Ardie, listen," she said. "You are made by a very special Friend, and that makes you special, right?" If she had been quoting the scriptures she would have used the word "created," but doctrinally she was teaching an eternal truth that makes all the difference.

You are special, and so am I. Hopefully we don't need an orange-and-brown hot pad to remind us of our worth—but if so, make one. Maybe you could even sell them! No, we can't buy our worth. We know the source of our worth—our eternal worth. We ourselves have been "bought with a price" (1 Corinthians 6:20). That's a truth to cast the doubt away.

IN THE MIDST OF STORM CLOUDS

Our Lord and Savior, our Redeemer, our Friend, Jesus Christ, suffered for each of us individually. He suffered for our pains, our heartaches, our disappointments, our feelings of inadequacy, our mistakes, our sins, and all our imperfections. Furthermore, we read in the scriptures, "He comprehendeth *all* things" (Alma 26:35; emphasis added).

President Ezra Taft Benson taught a truth I believe with all my heart: "There is no human condition, be it suffering, incapacity, inadequacy, mental deficiency, or sin, which he cannot comprehend or for which his love will not reach out to the individual."[4]

Despite this truth, we will continue to battle against the weaknesses of the flesh, and sometimes we will feel burdened as we fall short of our goals. When Oliver Cowdery began his labors as a scribe for the translation of the Book of Mormon, he was in need of reassurance. The Lord gave these words through revelation to Oliver, words that are important to all of us: "Verily, verily, I say unto thee, blessed art thou for what thou hast done. . . . If it had not been so, thou wouldst not have come to the place where thou art at this time" (D&C 6:14).

I fear too many of us carry burdens because we forget that we kept our first estate. We were the valiant and faithful ones, and our faithfulness has brought us to the place where we are at this time. We came with a mission, and when we are true to that mission, keeping our second estate for this brief time in mortality, we are promised we will have all the blessings God has to offer—everything. We will become joint-heirs with Jesus Christ (see Romans 8:17).

What wonderful promises! No wonder Alma calls it "the great plan of happiness" (Alma 42:8). When we have an eternal perspective we come to understand the reasons for the trials and tests of life. In the midst of the storm clouds we can come to rejoice as we understand the plan. In the words of Emily Dickinson,

> *We never know how high we are*
> *Till we are called to rise*
> *And then, if we are true to plan,*
> *Our statures touch the skies.*[5]

WE CANNOT MAKE IT ALONE

An explanation of why our performance falls short of our desires is found in what an angel of the Lord said to King Benjamin: "For the natural man is an enemy to God." Because we all become "natural" man and woman through sin, we will always have these battles until we yield to the "enticings of the Holy Spirit," and put off the natural man and become a saint "through the atonement of Christ the Lord," and become "as a child, submissive, meek, humble, patient, full of love" (Mosiah 3:19).

I am working on these attributes. Submissiveness . . . usually. Meek . . . hopefully. Humble . . . striving. Patience . . . can we just ignore that one? Full of love . . . having love, yes, but *full* of love?

Let this be our earnest desire. We read in the writings of John, "There is no fear in love; but perfect love casteth out fear: because fear hath torment" (1 John 4:18).

We cannot make it alone. If we think we can, we

deny the very purpose of the atonement and the sacrifice made in our behalf. Our performance might be likened to a two-year-old who pulls away saying, "I can do it by myself." Just as the two-year-old is incapable without the help of an adult, so are we incapable without Christ. Do we ever choose to not let the Savior come into our lives to pick up the slack at the end of every day and every hour because we are too busy, too tired, or too burdened with guilt or fear or doubt? Do we even wonder at times if he is there for us? If these thoughts ever cross our minds, let us hear again his tender words of love and promise and sacrifice for each of us: "Look unto me in every thought; doubt not, fear not. Behold the wounds which pierced my side, and also the prints of the nails in my hands and feet; be faithful, keep my commandments, and ye shall inherit the kingdom of heaven" (D&C 6:36–37).

His words of invitation and promise are repeated over and over in the scriptures: "Come, follow me"; "Come unto me"; "I am your advocate with the Father"; "[I am] pleading your cause"; "I have graven thee upon the palms of my hands"; "[I have] descended below them all"; "I am the good Shepherd"; "I . . . am thy Savior, and thy Redeemer"; "You are my friends." "Greater love hath no man than this, that a man lay down his life for his friends" (Luke 18:22; Matthew 11:28; D&C 110:4; 45:3; Isaiah 49:16; D&C 122:8; 50:44; 1 Nephi 21:26; D&C 93:45; John 15:13).

> *How great the wisdom and the love*
> *That filled the courts on high*
> . *And sent the Savior from above*
> *To suffer, bleed, and die!*
> *His precious blood he freely spilt;*
> *His life he freely gave,*
> *A sinless sacrifice for guilt,*
> *A dying world to save.*[6]

I wish I could speak to each of you with the same intensity and fervor with which my niece Shelly addressed me. I would call you each by name and say, "Brenda, Martha, Susan, Michelle, Brent, Kevin, Josh, Alex—now think, you are created by a very special person and that makes you special, right?"

> *I tremble to know that for me he was crucified,*
> *That for me, a sinner, he suffered, he bled and*
>   *died.*
> *Oh, it is wonderful that he should care for me*
> *Enough to die for me!*
> *Oh, it is wonderful, wonderful to me!*[7]

There are times when that assurance is absolutely essential to our survival. It is essential if we are to move forward and fulfill our foreordained mission. To each of you I say that you are better than you think you are—and with our Savior's help, you can be better yet. He is counting on each one of us.

HE KNOWS YOU; HE LOVES YOU

When I was called by the prophet twenty years ago to serve as the Young Women General President, all my weaknesses and imperfections and inadequacies loomed before me. I'm sure that feeling is not unfamiliar to many of you in relation to calls you have received. Did the prophet know I had failed a grade in school? Did he know I failed freshman English? Did he know I didn't have any children, so I could not be a good role model for the young women? Did he know about all my shortcomings and my insecurities? Did he know I was raised in a town of three hundred people and got lost on my way to school the first day at Brigham Young High School?

I prayed like I had never prayed before. I learned anew that our Father in Heaven knows us, knows all of our weaknesses, and promises that he will make weak things become strong when we humble ourselves and have faith (see Ether 12:27). As I was struggling with that weighty new call, I read these words in answer to my earnest prayers: "Cry unto God for all thy support; yea, . . . counsel with the Lord in all thy doings, and he will direct thee for good" (Alma 37:36–37).

Some of my most earnest prayers have been answered only after returning to my knees again and again, and sometimes the answer has simply been a feeling of peace while I learned to wait upon the Lord. A much-loved hymn says, "Prayer is the soul's sincere desire, uttered or unexpressed."[8] We all have difficult times when "we know not what we should pray for"; in those times "the Spirit . . . maketh intercession for us" (Romans 8:26). Our Savior is our advocate with the Father and pleads our cause (see D&C 45:3–5). Think of that. Happiness and fulfillment in this life is not an insurmountable challenge. The Prophet Joseph Smith taught, "Happiness is the object and design of our existence."[9]

The first step to happiness is sometimes as simple as "finding oneself." I'm reminded of an old story where a rather serious man said "Good morning" to his younger friend and asked, "So how did you find yourself this morning?" The younger man said with a grin,

"I just threw back the covers and there I was." Unfortunately, the sobering reality is that some people haven't found themselves, whether it is under the covers or anywhere else. They don't even know where to look. People tend to look for themselves in the labels created by others—to look at position, title, or prestige and think that that is their identity. And when it is threatened or changed in some way, they become lost.

Looking for outward recognition to provide a feeling of happiness can be very fleeting. In 1987 the town of Cardston, Alberta (population 3,000), was celebrating the centennial of the Saints' arrival in the area, establishing what would become a stronghold of the Church. President Ezra Taft Benson had agreed to serve as the grand marshal and lead the parade. Bishop Victor Brown, who was the Presiding Bishop of the Church and who had lived much of his early life in the area, was invited to participate. As Young Women General President, I was also invited to return to the place of my birth and ride in the parade. Bishop Brown and I shared a love for horses. He suggested that we each get a horse and ride together in the parade. I was honored by the suggestion, but explained to Bishop Brown that everyone in the area remembered me as a kid on a horse. I wanted to return as a lady in a carriage. He encouraged me in my desire.

Cardston has a provincial museum of elegant carriages, including one carriage that had actually been used by the queen of England when she visited an area north of Cardston. Several of the carriages were going to be used in the parade. I was notified that I and Sister Elaine Jack, who was a counselor in the Young Women General Presidency at the time and who had also grown up in the area, were to ride in one of these lovely carriages. I was excited.

On the morning of the parade the usual wind was blowing, but we were used to that. The beauty of the carriage was heightened by the team of beautiful black horses with fancy polished harnesses and by the drivers in black suits and high silk hats. Elaine and I climbed into the carriage and took our seats. We sat tall and straight, with as much dignity as two country girls returning home could muster. Sister Jack was born and raised in the town of Cardston. My home was twenty miles away in Glenwood, which had a population of approximately 250 people. When I was growing up, the thought of a Glenwood girl riding in a parade down Main Street in Cardston with a Cardston girl would never have crossed my mind, even in my wildest imagination. Yet here we were.

A large sign had been mounted on each side of the carriage, giving our identities and Church positions. We chatted briefly about the fun of returning home after all these years and riding in a carriage down Main Street in the Cardston parade. Shortly after the parade began, our carriage pulled around the corner of Main Street just as a huge gust of wind joined the occasion. It blew as only the wind in southern Alberta can blow, and in the process it tore both signs loose from the carriage and carried them away into the crowd.

Right at that moment, the young man on the microphone, who was giving identification and recognition to the entries in the parade, spoke above the sound of the wind: "I don't know who these ladies are, but they must be someone important."

That deflated us some. We didn't sit quite so tall after that as we joked together about the important lesson that titles and positions are temporary and can blow away at any time.

We don't need physical signs to help us remember who we really are. As members of The Church of Jesus Christ of Latter-day Saints, we are more than children of God. Through our baptismal covenants we are his *covenant* children (see Mosiah 5:7). We must be different from the rest of the world. Our identity is different. Our direction is different. And our purpose is different. Self-acceptance, knowing who we are, is essential to our sense of well-being. Our worth is God-given. In the words of Michael McLean:

> *She doesn't know*
> *That she's an angel in disguise*
> *And she doesn't know that*
> *We see heaven in her eyes*
> *And she doesn't know that she's all right*
> *She might have been blinded by the light*
> *Of all of the good that she does*
> *But she doesn't see it because . . .*
>
> *She hits a traffic jam on a carpool morn*
> *And feels guilty what she's thinkin' as she honks*
>   *her horn*
> *She wrote a sympathy note for her dear friend*
>   *Grace*
> *But got it lost somewhere in cyberspace*
> *And at the charity auction when she wanted to*
>   *help*
> *She raised her hand so many times she sort of*
>   *bid against herself*

She got the casserole made for her friend who
    was sick
But then apologized because the crust was too
    thick
She's runnin' to the soccer and the baseball
    games
She cheers for the teams but forgets their names
She doesn't know that she's a miracle
She doesn't know her love is lyrical
She doesn't know this song's for her to hear
She doesn't know that we are so sincere
She doesn't know that she's the best
She doesn't know she's passed the test
She doesn't know, she doesn't know,
She doesn't know![10]

"Enough and to Spare"

Remember the story in the Bible of Christ feeding the five thousand? His disciples asked a lad to give up his food—some fish and barley loaves—to feed the multitude. How do you think the lad felt about that? "You want my small lunch to feed five thousand people?" But Christ took the fishes and loaves and blessed them and there were several baskets left over (see John 6:8–13). There was "enough and to spare" (D&C 104:17). The miracle started when the boy gave all he had.

When we give all we have there is "enough and to spare." The problems arise when people hold back and think that what they have is too little or won't be accepted. We came with enough, and if we do our very best the Lord will make up the difference. With his help, we will measure up; we will be enough to fulfill our foreordained missions as sons and daughters of God.

We each do have a mission, a reason for being. Consider the words of President George Q. Cannon: "God has chosen us out of the world and has given us a great mission. I do not entertain a doubt myself that we were selected and foreordained for the mission before the world was, that we had our parts allotted to us in this mortal state of existence, as our Savior had His assigned to Him. I testify that when we give our very best, a kind Father in Heaven will magnify us and we will each measure up and fill the measure of our creation."[11]

As we face the future at this remarkable time in Church history, we can do so without doubt and without fear, but with joy and happiness. Hear these comforting words from a loving Savior: "Fear not, little children, for you are mine, and I have overcome the world, and you are of them that my Father hath given me; and none of them that my Father hath given me shall be lost. And the Father and I are one. I am in the Father and the Father in me; and inasmuch as ye have received me, ye are in me and I in you. Wherefore, I am in your midst, and I am the good shepherd, and the stone of Israel. He that buildeth upon this rock shall never fall" (D&C 50:41–44). We will not find ourselves under the covers, but rather under the covenant.

My people must be tried in all things, that
they may be prepared to receive the glory that
I have for them, even the glory of Zion.
—Doctrine and Covenants 136:31

AWAY AT SCHOOL

There are reasons for our tests. They
are part of the curriculum, the plan
to prepare us for graduation.

When we left our heavenly home to come away to this earthly school, we knew there would be some difficult lessons, hard tests, and times of homesickness, loneliness, and discouragement. We knew that if we were left to ourselves we would experience failure. We knew we could not pass the grade or meet the requirements for graduation without help. The fact is, the Lord never stops loving us or desiring to help us and bless us. In the words of Isaiah, "For I the Lord thy God will hold thy right hand, saying unto thee, Fear not; I will help thee" (Isaiah 41:13). We could not be an honor student or even an average student on our own.

We were assured that we would not be left alone, that "the Comforter, which is the Holy Ghost, whom the Father will send in my name, he shall teach you all things, and bring all things to your remembrance, whatsoever I have said unto you. Peace I leave with you, my peace I give unto you: not as the world giveth, give I unto you. Let not your heart be troubled, neither let it be afraid" (John 14:26–27). We knew that if we would listen and follow the guidance given us through the Holy Ghost, we would one day graduate with honors and with a degree, the highest degree in the celestial kingdom.

We knew that there would be many tests, each one for a reason. The Lord said, "My people must be tried in all things, that they may be prepared to receive the glory that I have for them, even the glory of Zion" (D&C 136:31). There is a reason for our tests. They are part of the curriculum, the plan to prepare us for graduation.

If we are to be tried in all things, should we not expect some feelings of anxiety when we feel pushed and rushed, with not enough time to do it all? Many of us understand the feeling of cramming for finals at school. Should we be surprised when we experience some stress from this course of study? We want to accomplish more and more, to do better and be better. And yet according to our evaluation we are falling behind in some classes—not chemistry or statistics and economics (which I hated), but in our scripture reading or temple attendance, maybe our patience, our hours of service, our charity or pride, our lack of faith—which may cause us to wonder if we will be held back because of our lack of performance.

I remember asking a young girl in the third grade, who seemed to be blessed with an extra degree of confidence, "Are you the smartest one in your class?"

"No," she answered, "I am second smartest. But Brad is last smartest."

Some of us may see ourselves as last smartest in some of the classes of mortality and feel inadequate, insecure, and even dumb at times. But we must never succumb to the enticings of the adversary to question our worth, our capability, our capacity, and the resources available to us to pass all the tests that really matter. In fact, we can even pass with honors if we will call upon the Lord for help and follow his directions.

An Open-Book Test

It certainly helps that our test is an "open-book" test, with all the answers. When we study the text—the scriptures—we find answers to the problems we face. Scripture study opens the conduit for communication, and through regular scripture study we will avoid those pressured times when we find ourselves cramming for finals. There will be times when we feel the Spirit speak to us through the very words we are reading, often in answer to prayer. I know this from personal experience.

I will never forget the day or the feeling in my heart when a little boy about five years old, new to the area, knocked on the door of our home. I opened the door and he immediately identified his reason for being there: "Can your kids come out and play?" He waited for my response, one that I had repeated so many times to so many people, "I don't have any kids." The visitor squinted his innocent, little face, looked up at me in wonderment, and posed the question that I had not dared put into words. "If you're not a mother, what are you?" He turned and hopped back down the sidewalk.

With my back against the closed door I repeated his question again and again, "If you're not a mother, what are you?" I even asked that question in prayer. If I wasn't to be a mother, what was I to do with my life?

With that thought weighing on my mind, one day

I was reading in the Doctrine and Covenants and came to section 11, verses 12 to 14: "And now, verily, verily, I say unto thee, put your trust in that Spirit which leadeth to do good—yea, to do justly, to walk humbly, to judge righteously; and this is my Spirit. Verily, verily, I say unto you, I will impart unto you of my Spirit, which shall enlighten your mind, which shall fill your soul with joy; and then shall ye know, or by this shall you know, all things whatsoever you desire of me, which are pertaining unto things of righteousness, in faith believing in me that you shall receive."

On that occasion, I put the date in the margin of my scriptures, reminding me that on that day that scripture became mine. That scripture became an important part of my personal preparation, a truth that is reconfirmed each time I read it.

When I was called to serve as the Young Women General President, I was anxiously searching for answers, for direction, for confirmation, for revelation, for comfort. I yearned to know more than I'd ever known before about how to listen to the Spirit and how to receive personal revelation. Again, I found two specific verses as a direct answer to prayer. I wrote the date in the margin next to those verses, along with the note, "the blueprint for finding answers to questions regarding Young Women." I thought that scripture was put there just for me personally at that time. I still think that.

However, on December 17, 1992, Elder David B. Haight was speaking at a mission presidents seminar in Vancouver, Canada, and referred to that scripture. In October 1993, Elder James E. Faust used this same scripture as a guide for mission presidents. So those verses were put there for others as well—but they are also mine.

The passage I refer to is Alma 37:36–37: "Cry unto God for all thy support; yea, let all thy doings be unto the Lord, and whithersoever thou goest let it be in the Lord; yea, let all thy thoughts be directed unto the Lord; yea, let the affections of thy heart be placed upon the Lord forever.

"Counsel with the Lord in all thy doings, and he will direct thee for good; yea, when thou liest down at night lie down unto the Lord, that he may watch over you in your sleep; and when thou risest in the morning let thy heart be full of thanks unto God; and if ye do these things, ye shall be lifted up at the last day."

The scriptures were recorded and translated as a guide for our day at an enormous cost. But if we fail to read them, that price was paid in vain, at least as far as we are concerned. The following lines from an unknown author suggest some caution about how the scriptures might or might not be used.

> *On the table side by side*
> *the Book of Mormon and the* TV GUIDE.
> *One is well worn and cherished with pride*
> *Not the Book of Mormon, but the* TV
>   GUIDE.
> *One is used daily to help folks decide,*
> *Not the Book of Mormon, but the* TV
>   GUIDE.
>
> *As pages are turned, what shall we see?*
> *Oh what does it matter, turn on the TV.*
> *So they open the book from which they confide*
> *Not the Book of Mormon, but the* TV
>   GUIDE.
>
> *The word of God is seldom read*
> *Maybe a verse here or there before they fall into*
>   *bed.*
> *Exhausted and sleepy, tired as can be*
> *Not from reading the Book of Mormon, but*
>   *from watching TV.*
> *So back to the table, side by side*
> *The Book of Mormon and the* TV GUIDE.

> *The plan of salvation is full and free*
> *But found in the Book of Mormon, not the*
> *TV.*[1]

NONE SHALL BE LOST

We must take time to study the text if we are to prepare to pass the test. When we ponder the scriptures, it helps to have specific questions in mind, looking for specific answers. Then many, many scriptures will become ours in answer to our prayers and our earnest inquiry.

If we had an opportunity to talk face to face, I'm sure we could share times when we've both faced some hard tests. I'm not referring to algebra, economics, English, or history, of course, but to tests that take away for a time our feeling of joy and happiness, our optimism and anticipation.

Our Father has planned the courses best suited to our individual needs and our development, peace of mind, and happiness. We are not expected to be in graduate school until we have passed the preliminary courses. Consider these comforting words from a loving Savior: "Fear not, little children, for you are mine, and I have overcome the world, and you are of them that my Father hath given me; and none of them that my Father hath given me shall be lost" (D&C 50: 41–42).

On occasion, not often, but more than I would hope, I have heard good Latter-day Saint women make comments that indicate they question their individual worth. They doubt they are measuring up to the high expectations they have set for themselves. "I probably won't make it," they say. I don't know if such comments come after a day when they had a disagreement with their husband or a misunderstanding with a child or skipped family home evening or are behind in their family history activities or didn't get their visiting teaching done on time or got angry in a traffic jam trying to hurry home to pick up a child from a piano lesson in time to get another child to the soccer game. Whatever the circumstances, it is clear that when we take a tally at the end of the day, we will have failed some of our tests. It's a rare day indeed when we are a 100 percent, straight A, honor student.

But we can take comfort in the words of Elder Bruce C. Hafen when he said, "I sense that an increasing number of deeply committed Church members are weighed down beyond the breaking point with discouragement about their personal lives. When we habitually understate the meaning of the Atonement, we take more serious risks than simply leaving one another without comforting reassurances—for some may simply drop out of the race, worn out and beaten down with the harsh and untrue belief that they are just not celestial material."[2]

CALLING HOME

It has been my experience that when we pass one test and move on, the testing continues—and so does the joy and happiness. As we progress the answers come more rapidly, because we will have increased our ability to hear what is coming to us through the Spirit. When we call home in earnest prayer, the lines are always open. When we are in tune there is never any call-waiting, no voice mail to be picked up later, no delay.

Last week I dialed a telephone number beginning with 1-800 and seven more digits, needing some information. I heard a recording asking questions and giving instructions: "English, press 1. Spanish, press 2. Do you want billing, new service, reservations?" and on and on.

The instructions continued, "If you wish to repeat

this message, press the pound key. If not, press star, or wait for an agent. There are four calls ahead of you."

Later: "You have reached the voice mail of John Doe. I am away from my office, but if you will leave your name and number and a short message, I will return your call. Begin your message after the sound of the beep." The telephone was dead. No beep came. I held it to my ear, waiting for further direction. Finally it came: "If you want to make a call, please hang up and call again." I hung up in complete frustration.

Yes, I'd like to leave a message, I thought. I want to talk to someone. I thought of the telephone operator in my home town. Years earlier, when I called home from Brigham Young High School because I was so homesick, the operator, hearing my voice, called me by name and explained that my parents were at the temple and afterwards were going over to the Princes' home for refreshments. She offered to take a message or have them call me. Just hearing a human voice from someone who knew my name was all I needed at that time.

Today, more than ever before, we are surrounded by electronic equipment that can, if we let it, keep us separated. Even while we are within reach of each other we can be out of touch, the message not getting through. "I love you. I care about you. You are not alone."

But when it comes to prayer, the lines are always open. "I hear you." "What desirest thou?" And prayer is a gift we must take advantage of. Many of our blessings "are made conditional upon our asking for them."[3]

Years ago at a girls' camp in the high Uinta Mountains, I suggested to a group of happy, enthusiastic young women that before the end of their camp experience they might wish to go out in nature by themselves and "call home" in prayer. Young Becky Lawrence, at the next fast and testimony meeting in her ward, stood to bear her testimony. She spoke of going into the trees by herself, seeking her own sacred grove. She said she didn't know what to say in that special setting, since she routinely prayed each day anyway. She explained, "Since I didn't know what to say, I just said, 'Heavenly Father, do you know I'm here?'" She told how she heard the wind in the trees and opened her eyes to see the sun filtering through the leaves. She paused and with quiet confidence and testimony told the audience, "I just felt warm all over." Then she added, "You may not think it was anything, but I knew he knew I was there."

We might ask the question Becky asked: "Do you know I'm here?" And if we listen we might hear the question reversed, "Yes. But do you know *I am* here?"

There may be times when we want to pray and try to pray, but we're not sure what to pray for or even if we are getting through. We know the challenge we're faced with, but aren't even sure how to ask for help. At such times, perhaps more than any others, we can be greatly blessed by the comforting promise of Paul to the Romans. We read, "The Spirit also helpeth our infirmities: for we know not what we should pray for as we ought: but the Spirit itself maketh intercession for us with groanings which cannot be uttered" (Romans 8:26).

I know that when we pray to have the Spirit and strive to live worthy of the Spirit, the Holy Ghost will speak to our mind and our heart (see D&C 8:2). In the words of Parley P. Pratt, we begin to grasp the powerful impact of the gift of the Holy Ghost in our lives. "It quickens all the intellectual faculties, increases, enlarges, expands, and purifies all the natural passions and affections and adapts them by the gift of wisdom to their lawful use. It inspires, develops, cultivates, and matures all the fine-toned sympathies, joys, tastes, kindred feelings, and affections of our nature. It inspires virtue, kindness, goodness, tenderness, gentleness, and charity. It develops beauty of person, form, and features. It tends to health, vigor, animation, and social feelings. It invigorates all the faculties of the physical and intellectual man. It strengthens and gives tone to the nerves. In short it is, as it were, marrow to the bone, joy to the heart, light to the eyes, music to the ears, and life to the whole being."[4]

WHEN YOU DON'T HEAR THE ANSWER

If we are going to follow the Spirit as we take our tests, we need to know his voice. The scriptures give us invaluable direction about how to proceed. When Oliver Cowdery was needing direction, the Lord said to him, "You must study it out in your mind; then you must ask me if it be right, and if it is right I will cause that your bosom shall burn within you; therefore, you shall feel that it is right" (D&C 9:8). This gave me concern for some time, since I wasn't sure I had ever experienced this burning as it is described. Further study helped me understand that that verse was given in reference to translating sacred records. And while this principle can apply to other situations where we need personal revelation, we need to know that there are other scriptures that give us additional guidance in recognizing the Spirit.

In Doctrine and Covenants 6:23, for instance, the Lord spoke to Oliver Cowdery and asked, "Did I not speak peace to your mind concerning the matter? What greater witness can you have than from God?" When we inquire of the Lord and feel peace of mind, we can feel that we have been in communication, the lines are open, and we are in touch with home.

However, there will be occasions when we will ask and not hear an answer. Does that mean that we are out of touch or out of tune? Not necessarily. Sometimes we must learn to walk by faith, not knowing beforehand what we are to do; and with some decisions, either proposed course of action would be acceptable.

In the times when I don't hear an answer, the words of Brigham Young are most comforting: "If I ask him [the Lord] to give me wisdom concerning any requirement in life or in regard to my course or that of my friends, my family, my children or those that I preside over and get no answer from him, and then do the very best my judgment will teach me, he is bound to own and honor that transaction and he will do so to all intents and purposes."[5]

Elder Dallin H. Oaks gives us further clarification about answers to prayer: "Where a choice will make a real difference in our lives, obvious or not, and where we are living in tune with the Spirit and seeking its guidance, we can be sure that we will receive the guidance we need to attain our goal. The Lord will not leave us unassisted when a choice is important to our eternal welfare."[6]

A DAY OF GRADUATION

As we continue to progress day by day, facing the tests that are part of mortality, we need to learn to be focused. Brigham Young, a great teacher, provided instruction for our course of study: "The closer people apply their minds to any correct purpose, the faster they can grow and increase in the knowledge of truth. When they learn to master their feelings, they can soon learn to master their reflections and thoughts in the degree requisite for attaining the objects they are seeking. But while they yield to a feeling or spirit that distracts their minds from a subject they wish to study and learn, so long they will never gain the mastery of their minds. So it is with persons who yield to temptation and wickedness."[7]

After I graduated from Brigham Young High

School, I returned home to Canada. We were met at the border crossing by a customs officer. His question was direct: "What have you to declare?"

I wanted to shout, "I'm homesick. That's what I have to declare." I had graduated with honors and I was on my way home.

While graduation from high school and university is an exciting time, indicating significant accomplishment, we all look forward to another graduation of eternal significance. Late in his life, my father, who never had the opportunity to graduate from high school but was well versed in the scriptures, was in the last stages of stomach cancer. He spoke with excitement, enthusiasm, and anticipation about his graduation. He had taken the courses, the hard ones, and passed with honors. His day of graduation was not marked with a cap and gown, the symbols of the world, but he was prepared for his homecoming in the robes of the holy priesthood, and he was prepared to receive as his degree the highest degree in the celestial kingdom.

One day we will return from our time away from home, from the schooling that has prepared us for exaltation. In judgment, we will be asked what we have to declare. And then, as President George Q. Cannon has so gloriously written, "I believe that when we see our Father in Heaven we shall know him and the recollection that we were once with him and that he was our father will come back to us, and we will fall upon his neck, and he will fall upon us, and we will kiss each other, we will know our mother also."[8]

To every thing there is a season, and a time
to every purpose under the heaven.
—Ecclesiastes 3:1

CHERISH THE TIME

Have you stopped long enough today to catch
your breath and awaken your senses to the
beauties of this season?

*I*n my hometown there used to be a large sign at the crossing next to the railroad track. It read *Stop, Look, and Listen.* You couldn't miss it. The direction was very clear and presented in a particular sequence. First you were to stop. After complying with that simple directive you were to look both ways, to see what might be coming down the track. And as if that wasn't enough to get a clear reading to insure your safety, you were to also listen. You were to see if you could hear the possible sound of a train on the tracks in the far distance or the forlorn, unmistakable sound of a train whistle, which cannot be confused with any other sound.

In today's hurried world, some days we may feel like we are on a fast-moving train along an endless railroad track. Perhaps it might be a good idea to mount a colorful sign on your refrigerator door or some other conspicuous place: *Stop, Look, and Listen.* The sign will be a reminder to stop in your busy life, to look at the world around you and really see it, and to listen to hear the Spirit.

Have you stopped long enough today to catch your breath and awaken your senses to the beauties of this season? Did you look at the blossoms forming on the trees before they were gone? Not only did you *look*, but did you *see* the drenched and dripping apple tree after the rainstorm? Did you see the hand of God in all his creations for our enjoyment and beauty? Did you listen to the young birds as they returned to the feeders in the backyard that have been vacated for some time? When you listened, did you *hear* the sound of the magnolia warblers returning to your yard, which is also their yard?

Did you stop long enough to give thanks to God for eyes to see, ears to hear, and a life to live in this beautiful world?

Sometimes things are better than we think they are. We can particularly feel that when we unleash ourselves from self-imposed worries and demands for perfection and feel the exhilaration and renewal that can be found when we take time to live, *stop, look,* and *listen.*

What might the Lord be anxious to tell us in our mind and heart (see D&C 8:2) if we would stop the demands of the fast-moving trains in our lives and take time to listen? What might come into our view if we paused long enough to not only look but also to see?

"Don't Miss the Spring"

Many years ago I was a teacher in a fourth-grade classroom, where I learned a valuable lesson about this idea. Would you come with me for a few minutes as we are transported back in our minds' eyes to that classroom?

It was a Friday afternoon, the end of April, and nearing the end of the school year. As I slowly and nostalgically rested my eyes on each student busily engaged in his or her lessons, I knew where to look for the broken and chewed-off pencils, the dog-eared notebooks, and the clean, neat, and tidy desks. Over a period of many months and many, many hours, I had come to know and love these children, all of them.

As I looked at those students and sensed how fast the year had come and gone, knowing that this season had passed and they would soon be leaving the fourth grade forever, I began to wonder, What was the very best curriculum we could have for this moment in time? Were the assignments written on the board more important than witnessing new life in the spring-time together?

While pondering, I thought I heard the words, "Don't miss the spring!" But they had just returned from recess with their hot, sweaty little bodies and it was time to go to work. Still, as I looked at these students I loved so much, I just couldn't bear to push them to work on this beautiful spring day. I got up from my desk, walked over to the chalkboard, and erased every one of that day's assignments from the chalkboard . . . all of them. Then in a quiet voice I said to the class, "Please, boys and girls, lay your pencils down, put your books away, and follow me quietly. We're going outside. When you come, please bring with you the special gifts God has given each one of you."

While many looked puzzled, some curious, and others surprised, only Becky near the back of the room asked in a loud and questioning voice, "What are we supposed to bring?" I had the full attention of every student. I explained that in the springtime of the year there are sounds to hear, new growth to touch, beauties to see and even taste. We were going outside to experience spring, I said, and we were going to do it with the gifts of our eyes, our nose, our hands, our ears, our mind, and our heart.

Like birds freed from a cage, these children were released to the out of doors, even though it wasn't recess or lunch time. By my request, we did little talking. The students agreed to wait until we returned to the classroom to express their thoughts and feelings about spring, which they would do in writing. We remained away from the classroom longer than anyone expected, even longer than recess. But it was not like recess. The playground was very quiet, except for the sound of a few birds in the oak trees on the west side of the schoolyard. The fresh air became part of our springtime experience, as a slight breeze carried the aroma of the early crocuses that had pushed up through the soil to be on schedule for the season.

When we returned to the classroom that morning, the smell of the year's accumulation of chalk dust was more noticeable. The room was very quiet as the children, with paper and pencil in hand, tried their best to capture their experience on paper. I will never forget the lessons I learned that day, not lessons about arithmetic, spelling, or social studies but about something far, far more important.

I was interested in what Bradley would write about. I viewed him as one of the less able students. He had found a spot on the lawn near the sidewalk and hadn't moved the whole time. It looked to me like he was just daydreaming, staring out into space. I didn't suppose this had been a very profitable time for Bradley. But as I walked by Bradley's desk, he was anxious to share his writing. "I'll read it to you," he said in a quiet voice, holding up his paper so I could see it. I knelt at eye level beside his desk. In a tone of conviction and declaration he read the title of his work. "Blue." He then continued, "I like blue because it makes you feel like you are in a place that never ends. It is like a thing you can touch and go right through. It is clear and nice. It seems like you can fall right through blue."

I gave thanks that I had not prodded him to see what I saw. I had missed seeing what Bradley saw with his eyes, his mind, and his heart.

From the back of the room I observed Christine, with her matted hair, her faded dress (the one she wore almost every day, with the belt held together with a large safety pin), and her elbows chapped from lack of care. She motioned for me to come. I wondered what this child might have written that could be reflective of spring and hope. When I reached her desk I glanced at the smudged paper, worn through in one spot from too much erasing. Her simple message read, "I never knowed the world looked so good."

She looked up eagerly, awaiting my response. With tear-filled eyes and on bended knee by her desk, I looked into her face and saw a new smile, bordered with chapped lips. I saw a new light in her eye. I whispered, "Thank you, thank you, Christine. I never knowed the world looked so good either. You have taught me an important lesson today."

Christine had discovered that things were better than she had realized, and the smile on her face assured me she had discovered she was better than she thought she was. A child in a quiet moment away from the demands of the classroom had witnessed a marvelous discovery about her world, using faculties that had not been awakened like that before.

There were many discoveries that day that had been concealed until the chalkboard was erased and the schedule changed to provide an opportunity to experience a quickly passing season.

TAKING TIME OUT

We need to do the same thing in our lives. There is a need to erase the chalkboard of our schedules, step out of the classroom of our routine, and discover again and again how beautiful the world really is. There is a need to interrupt what's on our planners and take a little *time out*. Certainly this life has a multiplicity of demands. We have so many lessons to learn, and sometimes our chalkboard is filled with lists and lists of things that need to be done, with places to go to and things to do and see. But as we focus on the chalkboard, we miss the lilacs in the spring. They come and go so fast. *This* season, let's take *time out* to smell the lilacs and see the daisies. When we take time to lay our pencils down and look up from our books, even briefly, we will celebrate the temporary and cherish the time.

To cherish the time is to taste, feel, touch, and appreciate with all our senses each season of our lives—the spring, the summer, the fall, and the winter. Often in the winter time of our lives, the hard times, we stop long enough and ponder deeply enough to develop a deeper appreciation for other times and seasons. That is a lesson and a blessing we can take to every season.

It is also good to ponder on times past. We can

cherish and savor those precious, fleeting moments more completely when we take time out to do so.

In the play *Our Town*, written by Thornton Wilder, the main character is a young woman, Emily, who dies and is given the opportunity to return to earth and live one day of her life over again. She chooses her twelfth birthday. When the day begins, her first reaction is an intense desire to savor every moment. "I can't look at everything hard enough," she says. Then to her sorrow she sees that the members of her family are not experiencing life. Yes, they are living life, but there is so much more. In desperation she says, "Let's look at one another." She pauses, then says, "I can't, I can't go on. It goes too fast. We don't have time to look at one another. I didn't realize it. So all that was going on and we never noticed. Take me back—up the hill—to my grave. But first: Wait! One more look.

"Good-bye, Good-bye world. Good-bye Grover's corners. . . . Mama and Papa. Good-bye to clocks ticking . . . and Mama's sunflowers. And food and coffee. And new ironed dresses and hot baths . . . and sleeping and waking up. Oh, earth, you're too wonderful for anybody to realize you."

She looks toward the stage manager and asks abruptly through her tears: "Do any human beings ever realize life while they live it?—every, every minute?" Stage manager: "No. . . . The saints and poets, maybe—they do some."[1]

FLEETING MOMENTS

Hopefully, as Saints—Latter-day Saints—we will not miss the precious moments that will never return again, at least not in quite the same way. As I think back on fleeting, cherished experiences, I am grateful that I took the time to briefly record in my journal enough of the detail to allow me to relive the sweet experience again and again.

July 20, 1971

Shelly is two years old. Hooray! Yesterday I took my orals for my master's degree from BYU and evidently passed with flying colors, according to the comments of my professors. But more importantly, Sharon (my sister), and Shelly returned from St. Louis. It is impossible to express what a wonderful enriching experience it has been to have little Shelly's spirit in our home. Somehow it puts all things in proper perspective as one thinks of things so important, just to drop in and have Shelly come running full speed ahead with her arms outstretched in a great hug. And they are here to stay.

October 11, 1972

I finished the paper that was to be presented at the National Council of Women. I then met with the Presiding Bishopric and shook hands with our dear prophet, President Harold B. Lee, as I was leaving the office. Then on my way home I stopped to see Shelly! I lose my sense of well-being if too many days lapse without contact with that precious little girl.

August 3, 1975

It was so much fun having Shelly stay over. Around midnight she awakened and came to whisper in my ear, "There is a fly in my room. Can you come and sleep with me?" So of course I did, and sure enough the fly disappeared.

April 17, 1980

On Tuesday morning at 5:30 A.M. on my way to BYU, I stopped at Sharon's. All were asleep. I knocked gently on Shelly's bedroom window and waited. She peeked through the blind and ran to the door to give me a big hug. What a way to start the day!

May we cherish each and every day, even with its ups and downs, and protect ourselves from becoming consumed in what may sometimes seem like the big things, which might rob us of all the little things that are the very essence of life.

*And, if you keep my commandments and
endure to the end you shall have eternal life, which
gift is the greatest of all the gifts of God.*

—DOCTRINE AND COVENANTS 14:7

YOU CAN MAKE IT

THE LORD HAS SET THE TERMS FOR THE
REWARDS AND THE PROMISED BLESSINGS.
DISCIPLESHIP REQUIRES EFFORT, COMMITMENT,
ENDURANCE, AND FAITH.

*S*ome time ago my husband and I saw the IMAX movie *Mount Everest*. It was incredible. I can't get it out of my mind. This mountain in the Himalayas, on the border between Nepal and China, is the highest mountain in the world. It is 29,028 feet. The physical endurance of the climber was absolutely remarkable, almost inhuman. Each step, one above the other, seemed to extract every ounce of energy from every fiber of his body, as he pushed forward against great odds on and through storms, freezing temperatures, and treacherous terrain, with an unrelenting desire to reach the top.

There are a myriad of examples in our lives of what would appear to be impossible dreams—impossible until we come to an understanding of the reason, the motivation that sustains the effort to accomplish the goal. When we can grasp even a glimpse, even a small insight into the outcome of something very important to us, we can somehow develop the capacity, the endurance, the desire, the stamina, and, above all, the faith to accomplish it.

As I watched that film I kept asking myself, What is the drive that sustains that kind of dedication, determination, and commitment? As I have pondered the answer, I have come to believe the drive stems from visualizing the outcome in the mind's eye, anticipating the realization of the goal. When we do that, the price that we must pay to attain the goal can seem to be diminished.

I am impressed with the story of Florence Chadwick, who determined at thirty-four years of age that she would be the first woman to swim the twenty-two miles from Catalina Island to the California coast. She had already been the first woman to swim the English Channel in both directions.

One writer reported the experience: "The water was cold that July morning, and the fog was so thick she could hardly see the boats in her own party. Millions were watching on national television. Several times sharks, which had gotten too close, had to be driven away with rifles to protect the lone figure in the water. As the hours ticked off, she swam on. Fatigue had never been her big problem in these swims. It was the bone-chilling cold of the water. More than fifteen hours later, numbed with cold, she asked to be taken out. She couldn't go on. Her mother and her trainer alongside in a boat told her they were near land. They urged her not to quit. But when she looked toward the California coast, all she could see was the dense fog."

A few minutes later, at fifteen hours and fifty-five minutes, she was taken out of the water. It was not until hours later, when her body began to warm up again, that she felt the shock of failure. To a reporter she blurted out, "Look, I'm not excusing myself, but if I could have just seen land I might have made it." She had been pulled out only one-half mile from the California coast. Later she reflected that she had been defeated not by fatigue, not even by the cold, but by the fog. It had defeated her because it had obscured her goal and blinded her reason, her eyes, her heart.

This was the only time Florence Chadwick ever quit. Two months later she swam that same channel and again the fog obscured her view, but this time she swam with her faith intact. She knew that somewhere behind that fog was land. And she reached her goal.

WHEN THE FOG CLOSES IN

This earth life is not intended to be an easy climb, and the shoreline is not always visible. But when we believe the top of the highest peak is real and the shoreline (whatever the distance) is somehow within our reach, the effort will never be too great.

The Lord explains the reason for the climb. "We will prove them herewith, to see if they will do all things whatsoever the Lord their God shall command them; and they who keep their first estate shall be added upon; . . . and they who keep their second estate shall have glory added upon their heads for ever and ever" (Abraham 3:25–26).

On those occasions in our lives when the fog closes in and the climb requires a determination and commitment that may test our faith to the very brink and we wonder why the climb is so steep and the fog so thick, we may need to be reminded once again the reason for it all. The Lord gives us a glimpse of the reason we walk by faith. "My people must be tried in all things, that they may be prepared to receive the glory that I have for them, even the glory of Zion" (D&C 136:31).

President George Q. Cannon gave us further insight concerning the reason we don't see the shoreline: "If we could understand the glory we once had with our Father in heaven we would be discontented in dwelling in this condition of existence. We would pine for the home we left behind us. Its glory and its beauty, its heavenly graces and delights were of such a character that we would pine for it with that homesickness that men have some partial knowledge of here on earth."[1]

Is it any wonder that we should, on occasion, sense a quiet longing for home, a homesickness that we do not identify as such?

I don't suppose that we are getting "trunky" to return home, like some of our missionaries did during the last week or two of their missions, but we need to be sure enough about the grand and glorious return that nothing, nothing keeps us from climbing and swimming. To move it out of the metaphor, we need to continue studying and praying and serving and repenting and loving and forgiving and listening to the whisperings of the Spirit. That Spirit says, "Keep going; you can make it." We are never alone.

ENCIRCLED IN HIS ARMS

The Lord has set the terms for the rewards and the promised blessings. Discipleship requires effort, commitment, endurance, and faith on our part. The Lord promises, "Be faithful and diligent in keeping the commandments of God, and I will encircle thee in the arms of my love" (D&C 6:20).

When we pursue our most important goals in this life with our faith intact, we never go it alone. We never climb alone, never swim alone, never reach our goal alone. Even when we seek to fulfill the very purpose of our lives, we are not alone. His arms open wide to receive us and to help us.

The knowledge of our premortal life has been forgotten. A veil like the dense fog of the California coast has been drawn for a wise purpose. We cannot see the details of the mountain peak or the shore, either of that which came before or that which is yet to come. We see both only from a distance. But when we remember our origins, and when we come to a full understanding of the promised blessings associated with eternal life, we begin to commit everything we have or will have to reach the goal. Because of the atonement of Jesus Christ, our Lord, our Savior, and our Redeemer, we can reach our ultimate destination.

We can be encircled in the arms of our Savior's love and become joint-heirs with Jesus Christ. And we can receive rich spiritual blessings along the way.

In the Book of Mormon we read of that remarkable occasion at the temple in the land Bountiful when 2,500 people were gathered after the resurrection of Christ. The Savior spoke to that large gathering, extending an invitation to each to draw closer, just as he does to us.

"Arise and come forth unto me, that ye may thrust your hands into my side, and also that ye may feel the prints of the nails in my hands and in my feet, that ye may know that I am the God of Israel, and the God of the whole earth, and have been slain for the sins of the world.

"And it came to pass that the multitude went forth, and thrust their hands into his side, and did feel the prints of the nails in his hands and in his feet; and this they did do, going forth one by one until they had *all* gone forth, and did see with their eyes and did feel with their hands, and did know of a surety and did bear record, that it was he, of whom it was written by the prophets, that should come.

"And when they had all gone forth and had

witnessed for themselves, they did cry out with one accord, saying:

"Hosanna! Blessed be the name of the Most High God! And they did fall down at the feet of Jesus, and did worship him" (3 Nephi 11:14–17; emphasis added).

If you and I had been privileged to be there on that occasion and to thrust our hands into his side and feel the prints of the nails in his hands and feet and see with our eyes and feel with our hearts and realize the price paid for our eternal welfare, wouldn't the desire and commitment to follow him at all costs burn into every fiber of our being? Yet on that occasion those gathered were warned by the Savior as we are today: "Behold, verily, verily, I say unto you, ye must watch and pray always lest ye enter into temptation; for Satan desireth to have you, that he may sift you as wheat" (3 Nephi 18:18).

WE CAN REACH THE PEAK

We often face the basic, routine happenings in our lives without recognizing the vital moving force that accompanies our comings and our goings. However, like the ebb and flow of the waters on the shoreline, there come occasions of high tide when the power of faith is activated in ways that we recognize as miraculous, and these experiences become the fruits of our faith. Such occasions bear evidence of the realities of God and our relationship to him. It is then that we can draw deeply from a reservoir of faith that has gradually accumulated over years of learning and living, "climbing and swimming," as we come to know the Savior and follow him.

Jesus Christ is our advocate with the Father in this process, pleading our cause. "Wherefore, Father, spare these my brethren that believe on my name, that they may come unto me and have everlasting life" (D&C 45:5).

This is the testimony that assures us that the very peak of the highest mountain, however steep the climb, is within our reach. "And this is life eternal, that they might know thee the only true God, and Jesus Christ, whom thou hast sent" (John 17:3).

My grace is sufficient for all men that humble themselves before me; for if they humble themselves before me, and have faith in me, then will I make weak things become strong unto them.

—ETHER 12:27

MIRACLE OF MIRACLES

WHEN WE MAKE A DECISION AND BECOME TOTALLY COMMITTED AND PERSISTENT, THE IMPOSSIBLE CAN BECOME THE POSSIBLE.

In the town of Anatevka, the setting for the play *Fiddler on the Roof*, Tevye, the Jewish father, introduces us to the challenges faced by his family and his friends in the village, comparing them to a fiddler on a roof. Tevye recognizes that it is through his family's traditions that he is able to keep his balance and achieve his dreams, despite his sometimes precarious position. We are quickly introduced to Tevye's wife, Golda, and his three young daughters.

As the story unfolds, the challenges of mortality emerge in a fascinating, realistic way that is easy to identify with. At the close of the drama, when the villagers of Anatevka are forced to leave their Jewish community, packing their wagons and not looking back, the similarities with the Mormon pioneers has been the emotional climax of the play for me.

But when I recently saw the play again, the story of Motel, the young tailor, became the focus. Motel appears on stage as a hesitant young man lacking in confidence, with low self-esteem, and conveying a feeling of worthlessness. He appears to be intimidated by many of the villagers in Anatevka. When he falls in love with one of Tevye's daughters, the realization that she also loves him fuels a new desire within Motel. He begins to dare to reach beyond himself and to develop the courage to ask her father for her hand in marriage. After several attempts to muster the courage, he finally, driven by intense desire but still hesitant, shaking, and trembling with doubt and fear, approaches the father to make his request known.

Until this moment in time he sees himself only as a poor tailor. But when he exercises his ultimate courage and makes a commitment, his deep desire ignites the light within him, and a mighty change begins to take place within his mind. He feels elevated, magnified. He immediately acknowledges God's hand in his life, not only as a miracle but as "the greatest of all God's miracles." He begins to sing. He sings of the miracles of Daniel in the lions' den, David slaying Goliath, the walls of Jericho coming down, and the parting of the Red Sea.

Standing tall with a new and almost unbelievable discovery about himself, he bares his soul in testimony and song.

> *But of all God's miracles, large and small,*
> *The most miraculous one of all*
> *Is that out of a worthless lump of clay,*
> *God has made a man today!*
> *Wonder of wonders, miracle of miracles,*
> *God took a tailor by the hand,*
> *Turned him around, and miracle of miracles,*
> *Led him to the Promised land. . . .*
>
> *But of all God's miracles, large and small,*
> *The most miraculous one of all*
> *Is the one I thought could never be:*
> *God has given you to me!*[1]

His greatest desire was realized—but not until he broke through the chains that held him captive. Those chains were his feelings of inferiority and inadequacy.

Once he was no longer held captive, doors began to open. He discovered life held possibilities that before he had hardly dared to dream of. His commitment to press forward released him to move onward and upward with unimaginable possibilities—including a first-time ever sewing machine for his work. His horizon changed. His life was different.

Our Limitless Possibilities

In some respects, we can all identify with the timid tailor as we encounter our own feelings of inadequacy. We fail at times to grasp the significance of our unlimited possibilities. When we become committed to do our best, give it all we've got, and trust in the Lord, we become future oriented and live in anticipation.

The words of George Q. Cannon help expand the vision of our possibilities. "We are the children of God, and as His children there is no attribute we ascribe to Him that we do not possess, though they may be dormant or in embryo."[2]

When we make a decision and become totally committed and persistent, the impossible can become the possible. President Heber J. Grant spoke often of persistence. "Persistence in the pursuit of righteous desires can help us develop talents, and attain our spiritual goals, and serve others."[3]

W. H. Murray wrote of commitment by saying: "Until one is committed there is hesitance, the chance to draw back, always ineffectiveness. Concerning all acts of initiative (and creation) there is one elementary truth, the ignorance of which kills countless ideas and splendid plans: that the moment one definitely commits oneself, then providence moves too. All sorts of things occur to help one that would never otherwise have occurred. A whole stream of events issue from the decision, raising in one's favor all manner of unforeseen incidents and meetings and material assistance, which no man could have dreamt would come his way."[4]

The words of Ryan S. Sheperd, a former Broadway performer now on his way to Harvard dental school, speak of one's possibilities. "People sell themselves short and don't think they're capable of achieving their wildest dreams," he says. "But I think if we're children of God and he is infinite, then our potential is limitless."[5]

Commitment to righteous goals, coupled with persistence, will take us to our greatest possibilities.

The Impossible Becomes Possible

As a young girl I was impressed by a book, which was later given to me, titled *Branches That Run over the Wall*. It was written by my grandfather's sister, Louisa L. Greene Richards. Lula, as she was called, became the first editor, from 1872 to 1914, of the *Women's Exponent*.[6] As I thought of my very own great-aunt as an author, I thought, "What a remarkable thing it would be to write a book!" I never spoke of the idea aloud. With my credentials, how could I ever even consider such a thing? Due to illness that kept me out of school much of the time in the eleventh grade, I missed out on many basic classes, including English grammar. In college I was once again reminded of my inadequacy when I failed freshman English.

Years later, after having completed a master's degree (though not in English!), I remember walking by the Deseret Book store in downtown Salt Lake City and imagining in my mind the satisfaction an author must feel to see his or her name on a book in the window or on the shelf of Deseret Book. At that time I had not even seriously considered such a possibility. Why would I? How could I? But what if . . . ?

At that time there were many books on the shelves for youth written by favorite authors, including Elders

Vaughn J. Featherstone, Marion D. Hanks, and Paul H. Dunn. But the problem, as I saw it, was that as good as those books were, they were directed more to young men than young women. I felt we needed motivational stories for young women.

While I was serving as a counselor to Ruth Funk, who was the Young Women General President of the Church at that time, I approached Eleanor Knowles, the editor at Deseret Book, with the concern. I expressed my thoughts. We need books for young women about young women, with stories that motivate, inspire, and elevate the goodness of young women.

I shall never ever forget her quick response. "Why don't you write one?"

I was taken by complete surprise. "Me write a book?" I said. I then began to justify my response. I recalled my failures and lack of grammar expertise. I tried to explain my problem. "I don't know a preposition from a dangling participle," I said, using that as firm evidence of the impossibility of the idea.

Eleanor just smiled and gave words of encouragement. "We have editors," she explained. "You just write the messages, and we can take it from there."

Really, I thought, *is this a possibility?* I told Eleanor I would think about it. I left her office with a thought burning in my mind.

With reservation and some hesitation I mentioned to my husband, Heber, the conversation I had had with the editor at Deseret Book. Instead of acting surprised or giving any indication of discouragement or doubt about such a possibility, he fueled the fire of desire within by offering a challenge. Since he was a builder of many homes, he challenged my competitive spirit with these words: "I'll bet you that I can draw the house plans, build a house, and sell it before you can write a book and get it published."

I had seen all the lovely homes he had built, but I had never seen a book I had written or even thought of writing. But the challenge generated within me an excitement over the possibility. A thought flowed into my mind: "I must not let any failures of the past hold my future in bondage." At that moment, I made a commitment to write a book for young women. I felt a passion for bringing to young women stories about young women that would inspire them at this time in their lives.

Once the decision was in place, wonderful things began to happen. For instance, that very week, to my surprise, Heber came home with a beautiful roll-top desk and a bundle of yellow pads and pencils—and a couple of erasers, of course. After I got started I felt like the tailor in *Fiddler on the Roof.* I realized deep within my heart that writing a book would take a miracle. But I knew that with God's help miracles can happen.

Once I began, I could hardly keep up with the thoughts I wanted to write. It was like adding fuel to a fire that had never been ignited before. I wrote page after page, all by hand. It was exciting and exhilarating. I could hardly wait until I had finished a chapter to read what I had written and move on to the next.

My first book was called *Miracles in Pinafores and Blue Jeans.* It was made possible through the help of the Lord, some hard work, and the help and encouragement of Eleanor Knowles and the editor she assigned to work with me. It was published and became popular, and there was a second and third printing. Eventually it was published in paperback and even translated. What once was a fantasy had become a reality. There at the Deseret Book store was a beautiful window display that I could hardly believe.

The stories were about miracles involving young women. The inside cover flap included this marketing statement: "You'll thrill as you read about the perseverance and faith of a six-year-old girl who proved she was 'made of bricks,' the vision of some teenage girls whose horizons expanded and seemed limitless when they worked together."[7] I won the bet with my husband—but I'm convinced Heber scheduled his project so it would be timed that way.

The real miracle for me was to discover, like the tailor Motel, that with God's help miracles are possible. His help comes once the decision is made and the commitment is entered into. We all have gifts and talents, but many lie "dormant or in embryo" until touched by the spirit of commitment.

"To Every Man Is Given a Gift"

We are told through a revelation given to the Prophet Joseph in Kirtland, Ohio, "For all have not every gift given unto them; for there are many gifts, and to every man is given a gift by the Spirit of God. To some is given one, and to some is given another, that all may be profited thereby" (D&C 46:11–12). When one person's gifts and talents cause another to harbor feelings of inferiority, envy, and jealousy, the unique gift given to that second individual is left uncultivated. It is a sad loss when anyone fails to cultivate the plot of ground given them to till.

I cannot count the many times that a stranger has approached me with enthusiasm, saying, "Oh, Sister Perry, I just love your music."

I feel obligated to respond with more than a simple "Thank you." I smile and say, "No, I'm sorry you don't love my music. I am not Janice Kapp Perry. She is my husband's cousin, and I love her music too." Then to avoid embarrassment for a well-meaning person, I say with a smile, "But maybe you like my books." Soon we become acquainted as friends, and neither music nor books are the issue. Friendship is a precious gift we can all magnify as we comfortably acknowledge the gifts we don't have and give thanks for the miracles that are available to each of us.

As I ponder the gifts and talents we may or may not have, Ralph Waldo Emerson's words have added to my way of thinking: "There is a time in every man's education when he arrives at the conviction that envy is ignorance and imitation suicide; that he must take himself for better or for worse as his allotted portion: that though the wide universe is full of good; no nourishing kernel of corn can come to him but through his toil bestowed upon that plot of ground given to him to till. The power which is in him is new in nature, and none but he knows what that is that he can do, nor does he know until he has tried.

"What I must do then is all that concerns me, not what people think. This rule, equally arduous in actual and intellectual life, may serve as the whole distinction between greatness and meanness. It is the harder because you will always find those who think they know your duty better than you know it. It is easy in the world to live after the world's opinions; it is easy in solitude to live after your own. But the great man is he who in the midst of the crowd keeps with perfect sweetness the independence of solitude."[8]

It is while pondering in solitude that we are helped by the Spirit to discover the plot of ground that we must cultivate if we are to uncover and claim our gifts. And then we can watch the miracle unfold.

I know that I am nothing; as to my strength I am weak;
therefore I will not boast of myself, but I will boast of my
God, for in his strength I can do all things.

—ALMA 26:12

WHERE DO I FIND MY STRENGTH?

HE WILL LIFT US UP, AND WITH HIS HELP
OUR PERFORMANCE CAN BE NOT ONLY ACCEPTABLE
BUT REMARKABLE.

Do you remember a time when you might have been asked for a résumé or a transcript that would have a significant bearing on your opportunity to be accepted to a college, a company, or a position of leadership? In a résumé we list our strengths, our accomplishments, our experience, and any other evidence that our wisdom, our gifts and talents, our personality, our skills and attributes, and our dedication should edge out others who may be competing for the opening. And if we do edge out others and get the job, there is typically a sense of pride in our victory.

The Lord's way is not man's way. We do not submit a résumé or even a letter of recommendation for a call to leadership in the Church. We never apply, and when interviewed we may immediately feel encompassed about by reminders of our lack of qualifications, our weaknesses, and our limitations. There may be many who seem much more qualified, and yet we may "get the job."

Without an impressive résumé as evidence of our qualifications, we usually know we need help—but where do we turn for that help? When we accept a calling to be a leader in the Church, a door is opened to strength, power, and influence that we do not have on our own.

When my husband was called to preside over the Canada Vancouver Mission, a friend with some experience shared a story that had an element of truth in it, for me, if not for Heber. As the story goes, a new mission president's first response is an earnest desire to be the best mission president the Church has ever had. A few weeks into his calling he catches a glimpse of reality, and his desire is adjusted somewhat; now he seeks to be just *one* of the best mission presidents the Church has ever had. In time he stops comparing himself to other mission presidents; he just wants to do the best he can.

The story ends there, but I would add the following sequel: if we are to accomplish the work given us to do, it is not enough to just do the best we can. Instead, we must do the best we can as our abilities are magnified by the grace and strength of the Lord. That goes far beyond the best we can do by ourselves.

In his famous poem "Invictus," author William Ernest Henley may be admirable in his dedication and confidence, but he is woefully lacking in his understanding of his source of strength. The last verse of the poem, which addresses challenges of every kind, ends with these words:

> *It matters not how strait the gate,*
> *How charged with punishments the scroll,*
> *I am the master of my fate;*
> *I am the captain of my soul.*[1]

This poet will yet learn that he is neither the master of his fate nor the captain of his soul. In the words of King Benjamin, "If ye should serve him who has created you from the beginning, and is preserving you from day to day, by lending you breath, that ye may live and move and do according to your own will, and even supporting you from one moment to another—I say, if ye should serve him with all your whole souls yet ye would be unprofitable servants" (Mosiah 2:21).

IN THE STRENGTH OF THE LORD

With every new calling, we seek for instant qualifications to compensate for our limitations. As one of my friends explained at the time of a calling, "I want to learn as fast as I can before people find out what I don't know." Along the way, we will have ample opportunity to be stripped of pride.

This acknowledgment of our own inadequacies is an important part of our preparing to receive the strength that is available to us. Our kind Father in Heaven provides a curriculum customized for our individual growth and happiness. He promises: "If men come unto me I will show unto them their weakness. I give unto men weakness that they may be humble; and my grace is sufficient for all men that humble themselves before me; for if they humble themselves before me, and have faith in me, then will I make weak things become strong unto them" (Ether 12:27).

Our first step in gaining access to this strength is as simple as having desire. We should desire not to outshine someone else with our gifts and talents, but rather to have access to the strength of the Lord, which will lift us above our natural ability. When we know that on our own we can do nothing of any consequence, then we are ready to receive.

Elder Neal A. Maxwell asked, "Is there not deep humility in the majestic Miracle Worker who acknowledged, 'I can of my own self do nothing'? (John 5:30.) Jesus never misused or doubted His power, but He was never confused about its Source either. But we mortals, even when otherwise modest, often are willing to display our accumulated accomplishments as if we had done them all by ourselves."[2]

Part of our weakness is that we are mortal, in a fallen state. We are surrounded by the reality of mortality and are constantly held back by our limited ability. We draw upon the Lord when we yield to the enticings of the Holy Spirit and become as Saints through the atonement of Christ the Lord (see Mosiah 3:19).

Thus we are lifted up far beyond our natural ability. We realize that even our painful limitations and infirmities can be a blessing to us. Consider the insight Paul gained as he faced his leadership challenges: "And lest I should be exalted above measure through the abundance of the revelations, there was given to me a thorn in the flesh, the messenger of Satan to buffet me, lest I should be exalted above measure. For this thing I besought the Lord thrice, that it might depart from me. And he said unto me, My grace is sufficient for thee: for my strength is made perfect in weakness. Most gladly therefore will I rather glory in my infirmities, that the power of Christ may rest upon me. Therefore I take pleasure in infirmities, in reproaches, . . . for Christ's sake: for when I am weak, then am I strong" (2 Corinthians 12:7–10).

THE INVITATION AND PROMISE

In the chapel of the Bountiful Temple, just behind and above the pulpit, is the familiar picture of the resurrected Lord with arms outstretched, signifying that comforting, reassuring message and invitation, "Come unto me." That invitation is current, immediate, and always present.

One early morning as I sat on the back row in the chapel, waiting to take my place as an ordinance worker, I looked at the open arms of the Savior and considered the invitation that drew me in. At the organ was an elderly, white-haired brother, and the strains of "More Holiness Give Me" filled the room, while a yearning filled my heart.

> *More purity give me,*
> *More strength to o'ercome,*
> *More freedom from earthstains,*
> *More longing for home.*
> *More fit for the kingdom,*
> *More used would I be,*
> *More blessed and holy—*
> *More, Savior, like thee.*[3]

In that quiet moment of solitude, while I was reaching for more and gazing at the open arms of our Savior, into my heart and mind came the words, "All that I have is yours. Can there be more?" With the invitation "Come unto me" is a promise of everything else. All that he has is ours.

The scriptures provide a long list of God's promises to us, coupled with a record of remarkable events that give evidence that those promises are sure. A pattern emerges. Note that the invitation "Draw near unto me" is followed by a promise, "And I will draw near unto you." Another invitation, "Seek me diligently," is followed by another promise, "And ye shall find me." The pattern continues: "Ask, and ye shall receive; knock, and it shall be opened unto you" (D&C 88:63). We find our strength in our willingness to accept his invitation.

The strength he gives us is exactly what we need for the circumstance. Helaman wrote of his two thousand stripling warriors, who fought the Lamanites with such courage: "They had fought as if with the strength of God; yea, never were men known to have fought with such miraculous strength" (Alma 56:56). Keep in mind that these were young men without experience. They never had fought before (see Alma 56:47). This was not a call or an assignment they were familiar with. Yet they were successful because the Lord was with them.

David was only a youth when he went before Goliath. But he knew the source of his strength. Speaking to Saul, this young man declared with confidence: "The Lord that delivered me out of the paw of the lion, and out of the paw of the bear, he will deliver me out of the hand of this Philistine." Approaching Goliath, he compared the resources of the giant with his own: "Thou comest to me with a sword, and with a spear, and with a shield: but I come to thee in the name of the Lord of hosts, the God of the armies of Israel, whom thou hast defied. This day will the Lord deliver thee into mine hand" (1 Samuel 17:37, 45–46).

The strength of the Lord is available not only in our major battles against the enemy but also in our private battles against weaknesses and infirmities. His grace, this "divine means of help or strength, given through the bounteous mercy and love of Jesus Christ," is an enabling power we can call upon when we have expended our own best efforts.[4] This compensation for our weaknesses does not come at the end of life or even the end of the day, but at the end of our own best efforts.

Throughout my life I have been plagued, frustrated, and humbled by a severe lack of a physical sense of direction. It is so extreme that reading a map and finding my way to a speaking engagement is far more stressful to me than delivering the speech upon arrival. I'm somewhat comforted by the fact that my two sisters suffer the same problem. My sister Shirley explains gratefully, "I don't know east from west, north from south, or up from down, but I do know right from wrong." Maybe that's enough, when we know where to turn for further direction.

I have finally acknowledged that this is one of my handicaps, "a thorn in the flesh," an embarrassment, to say the least. But it need not be. Whenever I leave home it is always with the earnest plea, "Father, lead me, guide me, walk beside me, help me find the way." To some this may seem a trivial matter, but for me it is not. It is a literal and very real need.

I have recorded in my journal many, many accounts of times when I have pulled off the highway to try to get my bearings, only to receive help from someone out mowing the lawn, walking a dog, or doing some activity that would place them right where I needed them to be to give me direction. In one case where the address was incomplete, the map was complicated (of course, they all are for me), and time was running out, a stranger going the opposite direction rolled down his car window to offer help. I explained my difficulty and he called out, "Follow me." He turned his car around, drove to the entrance of the church parking lot, honked, pointed, waved, and drove on.

I share this illustration as evidence that when we are in the Lord's service, he will make up for our limitations. When self-reliance and self-confidence give way, our struggles open the door to a deeper understanding of Christ's condescension and his commitment to succor us, bless us, comfort us, and even pray for us. He is our advocate with the Father.

Surely he is the Good Shepherd who pleads our cause and adds to our meager offering all that is needed. Consider the lines from the beloved song "The King of Love My Shepherd Is":

> *The King of love my Shepherd is,*
> *Whose goodness faileth never,*
> *I nothing lack if I am His*
> *And He is mine forever. . . .*
>
> *Perverse and foolish oft I strayed,*
> *But yet in love He sought me,*
> *And on His shoulder gently laid,*
> *And home, rejoicing, brought me.*[5]

He will lift us up, and with his help our performance will be not only acceptable but remarkable.

THE ROPE AND THE HOPE

The first step when we receive a call to lead is not to prepare a résumé of our abilities but rather to acknowledge our inabilities. It is possible that we will enjoy many expressions of commendation and even notes of praise. If this happens, may we be humble enough to acknowledge our own nothingness and give thanks to the Lord. A great example is given us by Ammon, who enjoyed such great missionary success among the Lamanites. Can't you imagine a missionary's urge to tell everyone of such success? Wouldn't it be natural to write home and have it announced in the ward or, even better, in stake conference?

But listen to the words of Ammon: "I do not boast in my own strength, nor in my own wisdom; but behold, my joy is full, yea, my heart is brim with joy, and I will rejoice in my God. Yea, I know that I am nothing; as to my strength I am weak; therefore I will not boast of myself, but I will boast of my God, for in his strength I can do all things; yea, behold, many mighty miracles we have wrought in this land, for which we will praise his name forever" (Alma 26:11–12).

We do not glory in ourselves, but in our Lord. And when we serve without words of commendation or appreciation, even when such approval seems deserved, we remember the Master whom we serve, knowing it is his commendation that we seek.

One summer I attended a three-day youth survival camp where we were all expected to rappel over the edge of a mountain that dropped eighty feet to the canyon floor below. Many of the youth, mostly the boys, lined up eagerly to take their turns. Everyone stood with attention riveted on Brother Tolman, the instructor.

He began explaining the dangers, the need to follow directions, and finally the essential nature of how to use the rope to move from the top of the mountain to the destination below.

When my turn came, I asked for one more review of the instructions. I wanted to hear all of them again, what to do and what not to do. The ground below was not visible from the top of the mountain, which added to the uncertainty of stepping off the ledge with only the rope to hang on to. Hanging over the edge of the mountain, I was able to plant my feet firmly against the solid rock, with my body almost perpendicular to the wall in front of me. Slowly I inched my way down the mountain, listening for the reassurance of Brother Tolman's instructions from the top, even though I couldn't see him.

About halfway down, forty feet from the top and forty feet from the bottom, I paused and looked down. Taking a deep breath, I changed my perspective by looking up. It was then that I sensed the significance of the rope, the strength of the rope, the essential nature of the rope, my dependence upon the rope if I was to survive this experience. On my own, I could neither climb back up nor ease myself to the surface below. Without the rope I could do nothing.

In a mistaken display of self-reliance and self-confidence, I could let go of the rope if I chose to, at least with one hand. It would be there whether I chose to hang on tight or not. The strength of the rope, my lifeline to safety, was never in question.

I have come to think of that rope as being like our lifesaving covenants. It is in the ordinances and the covenants that are available to us only in the gospel of Jesus Christ that we are bound to him, that his strength is made available to us. If we hold tight, we shall reach our destination.

President George Q. Cannon explains this relationship: "When we went forth into the waters of baptism and covenanted with our Father in heaven to serve Him and keep His commandments, He bound Himself also by covenant to us, that He would never desert us, never leave us to ourselves, never forget us, that in the midst of trials and hardships, when everything was arrayed against us, He would be near unto us and would sustain us. That was His covenant, and He has amply fulfilled it up to the present time and has shown that we can tie to the promises that He has made. We have proved these things through experience."[6] He assures us that he is the rope and the hope, the rod of iron and the gentle master teacher who calls encouragement from above. Like Nephi, we understand where to turn for strength: "O Lord, I have trusted in thee, and I will trust in thee forever. I will not put my trust in the arm of flesh; for I know that cursed is he that putteth his trust in the arm of flesh. Yea, cursed is he that putteth his trust in man or maketh flesh his arm" (2 Nephi 4:34).

At a BYU–Relief Society Women's Conference in 1998, Virginia Pearce reminded us: "Success is an affliction to our soul unless we recognize the source of strength."[7] The Nephite dissenters and the Lamanites learned something of how strength can be lost as they tried to overcome their challenges and fight their battles: "And because of this their . . . boastings in their own strength, they were left in their own strength; therefore they did not prosper, but were afflicted and smitten, and driven before the Lamanites, until they had lost possession of almost all their lands" (Helaman 4:13).

"Freely Give"

Christ instructed the apostles to "heal the sick, cleanse the lepers, raise the dead, cast out devils: freely ye have received, freely give" (Matthew 10:8). As we travel through life, we will encounter others who need to be lifted, encouraged, and sustained. An event in the lives of Peter and John demonstrates how the strength we are given can bless those on our path. The book of Acts tells of a man who was carried daily to the gates of the temple to ask alms of those who entered. As Peter and John approached the temple, the man "asked an alms. And Peter, fastening his eyes upon him with John, said, Look on us. And he gave heed unto them, expecting to receive something of them. Then Peter said, Silver and gold have I none; but such as I have give I thee: In the name of Jesus Christ of Nazareth rise up and walk. And he took him by the right hand, and lifted him up: and immediately his feet and ankle bones received strength" (Acts 3:3–7).

Peter did his part: He reached out and took the one in need by the hand. And then the power given him by Jesus Christ blessed the one in need. Peter called upon the power of the Lord through the authority of the priesthood, but all of us can draw strength from the blessings poured out by the Master.

A few years ago I received a letter written by a thirteen-year-old girl, a patient in the Primary Children's Hospital. She had heard of a family who were suffering grave concern over one of their children and had penned this letter:

Dear Brother and Sister Doxey:

How is your family doing? My name is Erica Monson. I am from Ely, Nevada. I am in Primary Children's Hospital. I'm getting better. I know how hard things are for you and your family, even though I'm thirteen. I hope that your daughter Kristen is lucky and finds the right donor so she can hopefully live to be a young woman. If I was old enough to donate and wasn't on medication for my liver, I would see if I matched your daughter's type. If I could I would do everything to make it so she would be able to live. I hope and pray for the best for your family.

Love, Erica Monson

P.S. If there is anything I can do, please feel free to write to me.

The message of this letter bears witness of her faith. The offer to freely give of herself to save another is evidence of the source of her strength, a source she clearly recognized even at her young age.

It is in righteous nurturing, in giving, not gold and silver, but faith, hope, and love, that those in our care are lifted up and strengthened.

I stand in awe as I ponder the incredible spirit and endurance of a righteous woman, my husband's mother, whom I met only briefly on two occasions.

Her parents were immigrants from Holland, with very little in the way of material means. She married young and was filled with dreams of a long and happy life. At the age of thirty-two, with nine children ranging in ages from three months to fourteen years, she was left a widow when her husband died of tuberculosis. While destitute of any financial support—the government relief check of $50 a month did not go very far—she insisted on paying her tithing. She told the bishop who hesitated taking the money, "Look, $5 won't help me much and my family needs the blessings." A relief truck came to town once a month, providing staples like dried beans and rice for the needy.

To add to this test of faith and endurance, eight of the children and the mother contracted the dreaded disease. For the mother it was tuberculosis of the kidney. Except for the baby, who was taken from the home, the rest of the children had to care for themselves while their mother spent time in the tuberculosis sanatorium or in bed at home for most of her remaining years.

At one point, the doctors provided some hope when they recommended that the infected kidney be removed in hopes of preventing further complications. The family decided to go ahead with the surgery.

However, the trial and test of faith and endurance were to continue. The surgeon removed the healthy kidney by mistake, leaving this young mother with an infected kidney that constantly made her ill. The mother returned home and was in and out of bed for the rest of her life. She lived until two of her sons returned from their missions and died at the age of forty-six, leaving a legacy of faith.

As I had the opportunity to become better acquainted with this noble mother through the enthusiastic memories of her friends and neighbors, I marveled at her courage and faith. Speaking of Peka Kapp always brought a smile and some recollection of her great sense of humor; her happy, indomitable spirit; and her infectious laughter. Her son Heber remembers that the children managed for themselves through her love, encouragement, and guidance. He remembers, "She would lie in bed and read to us from Church magazines." He added, "She was always upbeat."

This noble mother, like so many other good mothers who freely give their all in different ways, could say like Peter of old, "Silver and gold have I none; but such as I have give I thee" (Acts 3:7). A legacy of faith is far more precious than silver or gold.

*But unto him that keepeth my commandments I will give
the mysteries of my kingdom, and the same shall be in him a
well of living water, springing up unto everlasting life.*

—Doctrine and Covenants 63:23

NEVER THIRST
AGAIN

WHEN WE DRINK FROM THE FOUNTAIN OF LIVING
WATER WE ARE PREPARED TO CARRY ON.

We know something about the problems related
to drought and the blessing of moisture. Think of your
lawn and flowers or even a wilted houseplant without
the blessing of moisture, and then remember the
restoration and renewed life that come after the thirst
is quenched by water. As a farmer's daughter, I grew
up with a very real awareness of the importance of irri-
gating our crops if we hoped to have a harvest. We
knew that water was not only important but crucial to
our welfare. I recall the early mornings when I would
go out with my dad to irrigate, and the dew on the
grass made our old boots look new. It was along the

banks of those irrigation ditches that bordered our alfalfa fields that I learned many lessons about the importance of water.

Elder John A. Widtsoe, a noted scientist who was a lifelong student of irrigation and who became an apostle of the Church, pointed out the great symbolism in irrigation. "The dry desert soil," he said, "contains nearly all the elements of fertility. All that it needs is the enlivening power of a stream of water to flow over that soil. . . . Is it not so in our spiritual lives? . . . When this being . . . is touched by the power of the Holy Ghost, . . . suddenly a man blossoms into a new life, new possibilities arise, new powers develop. . . . We [can be] transformed from ordinary men into new powers and possibilities."[1]

The Vital Necessity of Water

Of course, physical water is absolutely essential in each of our lives. A few summers ago we were stunned, sobered, and very sorrowful when the headlines for the *Deseret News* on Saturday, June 8, read, "Boys . . . Rush for Water in an Effort to Save Scout." The report continued, "Bountiful Scouts succumb to heat exhaustion after water runs out." (We live in Bountiful, Utah.) The article explained that a group of Boy Scouts, on a summer outing, had not counted on three days of record-breaking temperatures in the high Arizona desert. Heat surged to 112 degrees. One of the Scouts passed out less than a quarter-mile from the Colorado River. His friend reported, "David was about 100 yards away from the river when he collapsed and died."[2]

Our need for physical water teaches us about our need for living water. Do you know anyone who is only one hundred yards from living water who might be dying spiritually for want of that water, losing hope, giving up, overcome with adversity? In your own life, have you sometimes felt wilted, thirsting for lifesaving moisture to lift you emotionally and spiritually? Have we not all encountered paths along our journey that are challenging, with soaring temperatures creating feelings of increasing exhaustion?

The news article reported that two members of the group were found unconscious but were flown to a hospital and given water and proper care. With medical assistance they recovered. Are we aware of where to find a spiritual hospital, where we can be given water and proper care?

Along the report of the incident, the newspaper included a sidebar with the heading, "Additional Information—Survival Tips for Desert Hikers." As I read these tips, I saw that they are equally important for those wanting to survive the spiritual deserts that we must endure as part of this mortal journey:

"1. Take more than enough water. Drink at least a gallon a day, more during hot weather." How much is a gallon of spiritual water? Can we get it by just taking a sip from the cup? A cup might be enough if we think of a sacrament cup, taken once a week as a reminder of our sacred covenants. But a cup isn't enough when we think of the "fountain of living waters" we are all invited to partake of (see 1 Nephi 11:25).

"2. Pack all your water in. Don't depend on nature sources along the trail. You may be surprised." We need to be spiritually self-reliant. We need to take our living water with us as we journey through life. President Heber C. Kimball said, "The time is coming when no man or woman will be able to endure on borrowed light. Each will have to be guided by the light within himself. If we do not have it, you will not stand."[3] The same is true of water. We need to constantly carry with us the ability to partake from the source.

"3. Always hike with an experienced guide familiar with the area." As Latter-day Saints we sing, "We thank thee, O God, for a prophet to guide us in these latter days."[4] Prophets are wise and experienced guides. In addition, at the time of our baptism and confirmation, members of the Church are given an infallible guide—the gift of the Holy Ghost, who will direct us in all things. When we prepare ourselves to listen, we hear His whisperings in our minds and in our hearts (see D&C 8:2). When we ask and when we listen, it is as if we have our own liahona.

At the time of our baptism, in a symbol of living water, we planted our feet on gospel sod. At the same time, we began a journey that would provide for each of us tests, tests, tests. Some of the greatest tests come in the heat of the battle when the temperature is high, when Satan has marshaled all of his forces for war, continuing his premillennial struggle for our individual souls. Eliza R. Snow reminds us in her hymn "The Time Is Far Spent":

> *Be fixed in your purpose, for Satan will try you;*
> *The weight of your calling he perfectly knows.*
> *Your path may be thorny, but Jesus is nigh you;*
> *His arm is sufficient, tho demons oppose.*[5]

We will do well only in that battle if we have a good supply of living water.

When we think of how important physical water is,

that may help us to better see why we must constantly seek access to living water. Only in the gospel of Jesus Christ do we find the ordinances and covenants that give access to living water—living water that can quench the thirst of those who may be dying spiritually or just suffering from very real spiritual drought.

THE WOMAN AT THE WELL

In my home is a beautiful painting of the woman at the well in Samaria. When I go to the Bountiful Temple, I often reflect on two other impressive paintings of that scene. This same scene is depicted on a very large stone panel at the entrance of the Cardston Alberta Temple, the temple that is not far from where I was born and raised. Even before I had a temple recommend and could go inside, I would stand and ponder that scene. Why was that event so significant that it is depicted in prominent locations in many temples, maybe all of them? Who was this woman, I wondered, that the Savior would go out of his way to meet her at the well? What was his message then and now?

The account of Jesus and this woman is recorded in the book of John. Jesus was traveling through Samaria and, growing weary of his journey, sat at a well that had been built by Jacob, son of Isaac. While he was there, a Samaritan woman came to draw water, and Jesus asked her to give him a drink.

"Then saith the woman of Samaria unto him, How is it that thou, being a Jew, askest drink of me, which am a woman of Samaria? for the Jews have no dealings with the Samaritans." The woman didn't yet know who Christ was, nor did she know who she really was.

"Jesus answered and said unto her, If thou knewest the gift of God, and who it is that saith to thee, Give me to drink; thou wouldest have asked of him, and he would have given thee living water.

"The woman saith unto him, Sir, thou hast nothing to draw with, and the well is deep: from whence then hast thou that living water? . . ." She was being temporally focused, but Jesus wanted to lift her sights to an eternal focus.

"Jesus answered and said unto her, Whosoever drinketh of this water shall thirst again: But whosoever drinketh of the water that I shall give him shall never thirst; but the water that I shall give him shall be in him a well of water springing up into everlasting life" (John 4:9–11, 13–14).

Jesus then spoke with the woman about the fact that she had been married five times and that she was then living with a man to whom she was not married (see John 4:16–19). Finally, he bore testimony of his true identity. When the woman said, "I know that Messias cometh, which is called Christ: when he is come, he will tell us all things," Jesus answered, "I that speak unto thee am he" (John 4:25–26).

It is interesting that we don't even know the name of this woman. Perhaps in this way she stands as a symbol for all women and all men of all time, helping us to see that the Lord loves each of us no matter who or where we are. With all our weaknesses and imperfections, with our wrong choices and mistakes, as saints, sinners, and all in between, he will come to us with buckets of living water and bless us beyond measure.

This story tells us much about the importance of living water and how we may receive it. When we ask questions about a subject, we prepare our minds to receive answers. When we then listen and are taught by the Spirit, we gain a deeper understanding. Here are a few questions we can ponder about that remarkable occurrence at the well in Samaria:

1. What was the setting of Christ's important message? Did the fact that it took place in Samaria have any special meaning? Is it meaningful that it was a private conversation between Jesus and a woman?

2. What was the conversation between the woman and the Savior? Was it just a social visit?

3. What was the difference between the water the Savior offered her and the water she offered him?

4. What does it mean to never thirst?

5. Where do we get that kind of water? How much does it cost?

6. Where is the well of living water? Must we go to Samaria, or in fact is it right here?

7. Will we accept Jesus' offer of living water? Or will we, by our choices, suffer a dry and parched thirst and maybe be overcome with spiritual exhaustion just one hundred yards from the source?

8. Will we collect enough water that our children and family will not thirst?

9. Will we teach our families of the water so when we're not there they will be familiar with the source and drink freely?

10. Are there people in our circle of influence who are just one hundred yards from the water—people we might rescue if we would?

11. What was it the Savior wanted to teach the women at the well? What does he wish to teach all of us? Did she learn? Will we?

Who was this woman at the well, with whom Jesus

chose to share his message of living water and declare his identity as the Messiah? She was not a Relief Society president or a Young Women president. She was not the wife of a stake president or General Authority. She was a woman who had made many wrong choices. She wouldn't even have been allowed in the temple at that time in her life, since she apparently was living in an adulterous relationship. And yet she was the one we read of in the scriptures to whom Jesus gave his precious message about the living water, which represents the love of God (see 1 Nephi 11:25).

Today you and I are not at Jacob's well in Samaria. But it is not only possible but a reality of enormous consequence that we too can drink of that water that the Savior offered the woman at the well. We can feel his love this very day, and tomorrow, and the day after. We don't need water pots to catch and hold it. The water is running in such abundance that we are able to partake only a small portion. The supply is never in question unless we ourselves turn off the flow.

There are times in all of our lives when we, like plants in need of water, feel withered and are desperately in need of moisture if we are to survive. We may be thirsting for understanding or forgiveness or patience. We may be thirsting for acceptance or for friendship or for peace and happiness. We may be thirsting for reassurance. All of these things are offered through the living water that Christ gives us, and they can flow to us like a fountain.

GETTING THE WATER INSIDE

Once Heber and I visited the home of an eight-year-old boy, who greeted us at the door. His first question, with his eyes bright and with a sense of interest that seemed more than just curiosity, was this: "Have you ever shaken the hand of the prophet?"

I responded, "Yes, Brent, I have."

His immediate response revealed something of his inner feeling. "Oh," he said, "if I could only shake the hand of the prophet."

The impression that came to me at that moment was to reach out my hand and to say, "Brent, this hand has shaken the hand of the prophet."

He grabbed my hand, shook it with a tight squeeze. Then he looked at his hand and exclaimed, "I'll never wash my hand." As I considered the likely accumulation of a day's activities on the hand of an eight-year-old, I suggested that he just look at his hand and keep the memory. He considered for a moment, and then said, "I'll wash my hand," he said, "but I'll save the water." He left the room and returned quickly with a plastic bag dripping with water. In time, holding the bag posed some inconvenience. He then had another bright idea. He left the room and shortly returned without the bag. His well-worn T-shirt was wet down the front. He stood tall as he gave his explanation, "I drank the water."

That young boy wanted some permanent tie with the prophet. He wanted to get the water on the inside. Oh, what a powerful message I learned from Brent that day. The following Sunday at sacrament meeting, as those sacred emblems were being passed, I took the cup of water and put it to my lips. I thought I better understood Brent's desire to get the water on the inside.

The Well, the Woman, the Water, and Us

Do we catch the significance here of the well, the woman, and the water, and what that means to you and to me today? In our relationships, when the temperature is high, our great need is for living water and the Holy Spirit. If we would stop and drink from our canteens, we might prevent wilting, withering relationships. In the writings of Isaiah we read, "For I will pour water upon him that is thirsty, and floods upon the dry ground: I will pour my spirit upon thy seed, and my blessing upon thine offspring" (Isaiah 44:3).

This is the Lord's promise when the heat is on and the temperature of temptation is high and doubts and fears rise up in our hearts. The Lord wants us to develop within ourselves an access to his living spring that will quench our search for peace and happiness, both daily and forever.

Where do we find this saving water? Will we? We can be surrounded by water, especially living water, but until we get it on the inside it will do nothing to quench our spiritual thirst, even if our need is life-threatening. It might be like placing a bucket of water near a plant in the backyard. As the sun beats down and the plant begins to wither and die, its rescue is agonizingly close—but the water is of no value, even though it is very near the plant. The Prophet Joseph Smith taught, in essence, that you can have a milk pan without a pan of milk.[6] We could add that we can have a fruit orchard without having an orchard of fruit. There are some who may be in the Church but may not have the Church in them.

The Lord gives us a key to turn the tap as we make our desert journey through this earth life. In the Doctrine and Covenants we read how to tap into the well of living water that refreshes and enlivens our souls: "Unto him that keepeth my commandments I will give the mysteries of the kingdom, and the same shall be in him a well of living water, springing up unto everlasting life" (D&C 63:23). When we keep the commandments we are filled with the Spirit and with the love of the Lord, and then our canteens are filled. We are taught things essential for our journey, things that can be learned only by the Spirit.

We live in a time of great spiritual thirst. Many are traveling without water in their canteens, yearning for a source of refreshment that will quench their thirst. They may be only one hundred yards from the water, and yet without insight and knowledge they can find no comfort for their parched souls. The Lord tells us, "If any man thirst, let him come unto me, and drink" (John 7:37). In the Doctrine and Covenants we read, "Yea, if they will come, they may, and partake of the waters of life freely" (D&C 10:66).

Fruits and Roots

The key to obtaining the living water is to come unto Christ and obey his commandments. It has been said that if we hope to have the fruits of the gospel we must also have the roots of the gospel. The roots of the gospel are found in the ordinances and covenants. The fulness of the gospel itself is referred to as the new and everlasting covenant (see D&C 22:1). Part of coming unto Christ is to receive the ordinances and covenants made available through the restoration of the gospel of Jesus Christ. Then, as we continue in faithfulness, we have access to the living water that blesses our lives now and forever.

The Book of Mormon helps us understand the relationship between ordinances and covenants. Alma said at the waters of Mormon, after describing the expectations placed on a member of God's church, "Now I say unto you, if this be the desire of your hearts, what have you against being baptized in the name of the Lord, as a witness before him that ye have entered into a covenant with him, that ye will serve him and keep his commandments, that he may pour out his Spirit more abundantly upon you?" (Mosiah 18:10). An ordinance is a witness of a covenant.

In the gospel, the term *ordinance* also includes rules and commandments and procedures. "The atonement is the focal point of each saving ordinance."[7] Each ordinance of the gospel points us to Christ and his atonement—and to the living water that flows from him, the fount.

One day I arrived at Relief Society a bit late—not a habit, I might add—perhaps as a response to a spiritual prompting of which I was not aware. A dear sister, somewhat older than I and usually a happy, radiant soul, sat on the bench near the door outside the Relief Society room, her hands folded in her lap and her head down. I felt impressed to take a seat beside her. She looked up with tears in her eyes and a troubled countenance. She began to unfold the burden she was carrying. She had five children. Two had died, her husband was hospitalized with Alzheimer's, and she had serious concern for a son and daughter who were struggling with the consequences of having made wrong choices. Her heart was heavy. The burden seemed unbearable.

"Is there anything I can do to help?" I asked. Amid her tears, her usual smile returned to her lips as she raised both arms high above her head, then dropped them into her lap, exclaiming, "It will all come out in the wash." Oh, how true that is.

We sat together and talked about the wash, the waters of baptism, the cleansing power of the Holy Ghost, the sacrament, and our covenants with the Lord. We talked about the atonement and the temple, which stood only a few blocks from her home, and the sacred lifesaving ordinances found within those sacred walls. "Yes," she said, "it will all come out in the wash."

Because of the atonement of Jesus Christ, these blessings are available to us and will prepare us to return to the presence of our Father in Heaven. It is through the ordinances and covenants of the gospel that we have access to the cleansing and healing power of living waters.

LET THE BLESSINGS FLOW

There are great blessings that flow from each ordinance and each covenant. For example, the ordinance of baptism opens the gate to the celestial kingdom. We read of this gate in the writings of Nephi: "For the gate by which ye should enter is repentance and baptism by water" (2 Nephi 31:17).

It is the ordinances of the temple, however, that open the gate of exaltation. It is amazing to contemplate that there are now 119 temples where these blessings can be received. More than half of these have been dedicated since President Hinckley became president. Do we grasp the significance of this time and season in the history of the Church? Elizabeth Barrett Browning gives us this insight:

> *Earth's crammed with heaven,*
> *And every common bush afire with God;*
> *But only he who sees, takes off his shoes,*
> *The rest sit round it and pluck blackberries.*[8]

Could it be that we are distracted in picking blackberries and miss the magnificence of this time?

Of the signal importance of the temple ordinances, President Brigham Young declared: "Let me give you a definition in brief. Your endowment is to receive all those ordinances in the house of the Lord which are necessary for you after you have departed this life to enable you to walk back to the presence of the Father, passing the angels who stand as sentinels, and gain your eternal exaltation."[9]

Living waters flow from the temple. In Ezekiel 47 we read that Ezekiel saw in vision the temple that is to be built in Jerusalem. There he saw a spring of pure water that "issued out from under the threshold of the house" (Ezekiel 47:1). The spring became a river, which flowed through the wilderness of Judea, a dry desert area, and emptied into the Dead Sea. And there, "the waters shall be healed" (Ezekiel 47:8). Ezekiel described the powerful effect of the water in these words: "And it shall come to pass, that every thing that liveth, which moveth, whithersoever the rivers shall come, shall live: . . . because these waters shall come thither: for they shall be healed; and every thing shall live whither the river cometh" (Ezekiel 47:9).

This fountain of living water represents the love and knowledge of God that flow from the temple. We read further that Ezekiel was brought to the door of the house, and he saw that the waters flowed out under the threshold. He was taken outside the gate, where the waters were ankle deep. He continued and was taken out where the water was to his knees and then to his loins. Finally he said it was a river he could not pass over (see Ezekiel 47:1–5). What a powerful image of the blessings that flow from the temple.

When I was called to serve as the Young Women General President some years ago, we pondered the focus for everything Young Women should be about. First, of course, is the covenant of baptism, where we promise "to stand as witnesses of God at all times and in all things and in all places" (Mosiah 18:9). This is reflected in the first part of the Young Women theme. But if we are to have a sense of direction and purpose for life and avoid drifting and dreaming, we need to look beyond that initial focus to our ultimate goal, exaltation. This higher focus is summarized in the simple statement (the last part of the Young Women theme) that we will "prepare to strengthen home and family, make and keep sacred covenants, receive the ordinances of the temple, and enjoy the blessings of exaltation." That's putting our priorities for life in a nutshell.

When we do our part, we have the sure promise of all these blessings. The question is never whether the Lord can or will bless us. The question is, Will we resist the power of Satan and do our part? Hear the Lord's words: "I, the Lord, am bound when ye do what I say; but when ye do not what I say, ye have no promise" (D&C 82:10).

During a three-year period when my husband and I were assigned to the Cardston Alberta Temple, we were away from home. At that point we realized more powerfully than ever before that it truly is the temple that is our home away from home. The temple is the bridge between mortality and immortality. It is the place where we receive comfort, peace, vision, hope, and promise. In the temple we are reminded of our identity, including who we are and who we are to become, as we prepare to fulfill our foreordained missions on earth.[10]

This great, eternal truth is captured in the words of a little five-year-old. Her parents had made the covenant of baptism a year earlier, and now they had come to the temple with their little girl to be sealed as a family forever. Coming down the stairs from the room where these sacred ordinances take place, this child, in her little white dress, filled with the Spirit, announced to everyone present, "Now we are a family forever and ever and ever until I meet my love." The Spirit would yet teach her great eternal truths when she meets her love, and this family may carry on generation after generation. As we endure our desert experiences and drink freely of the living water made available through our covenants, the promised blessings come.

President Ezra Taft Benson tells us: "The temple will be a standing witness that the power of God can stay the powers of evil in our midst. Many parents in and out of the Church are concerned about protection against a cascading avalanche of wickedness which threatens to engulf the world. There is a power associated with the ordinances of heaven, even the power of godliness, which can and will thwart the forces of evil if we will be worthy of those sacred covenants made in the temple of the Lord. Our families will be protected, our children will be safeguarded as we live the gospel, visit the temple, and live close to the Lord."[11]

THE VISION OF THE OTHER SIDE

Through our temple covenants, we gain an eternal perspective and realize the purpose of life. When the Savior visited the Nephites at the temple in the land Bountiful, he perceived that the people did not understand all he was wanting to teach them. Concerned for their spiritual progress, he gave them five keys or steps to accelerate their spiritual development. He said to them—as he says to us each time we return to his house—"I perceive that ye are weak, that ye cannot understand all my words which I am commanded of the Father to speak unto you. . . . Therefore, (1) go ye unto your homes, and (2) ponder upon the things which I have said, and (3) ask of the Father, (4) in my name, that ye may understand, and (5) prepare your minds for the morrow, and I come unto you again" (3 Nephi 17:2–3; numbering added).

Our Savior will come to us when we seek him. The temperature in our lives may be life-threatening because of the soaring heat, or we may be struggling in the severe cold, but his arms of mercy will reach out to every soul, even in the most challenging of circumstances.

In the early history of the Church, the Saints, including Joseph and Emma Smith, were already facing cruel persecution. Joseph had suffered violence on more than one occasion and had been falsely arrested. In early 1831, Joseph and Emma lost twins the same day they were born. They adopted twins whose mother had died, but less than a year later one of the twins died from exposure when a mob attacked Joseph, nearly killing him. Knowing all this was coming, still the Lord said to Emma in 1830, "Lift up thy heart and rejoice, and cleave unto the covenants which thou hast made" (D&C 25:13).

There is a connection between cleaving to our covenants and rejoicing. We can find comfort in our covenants throughout our journey of life. After more than six decades of marriage, President Hinckley wrote a special letter to his beloved wife, Marjorie. It includes this tender message: "My darling, It is now more than sixty years since we entered the Salt Lake Temple, there to be married for eternity." At the close of the letter he adds, "And when in some future day the hand of death gently touches one or the other of us there will be tears, yes, but there will also be a quiet and certain assurance of reunion and eternal companionship."[12] That promise comes with our sealing covenants. What greater blessing could we ever hope for?

As we close this chapter, I would like to invite you to join with me in visualizing a scene by an irrigation ditch. One particular morning, when my father and I worked through our alfalfa field and stood side by side at the edge of a main irrigation ditch, Dad took the shovel from his shoulder and made his way down the bank of the ditch to the water's edge. Then he turned and, with one foot high on the bank, stretched his hand toward me. Taking my hand in his, he steadied me until we stood together near the precious water. "We're going to vault across the ditch," he explained. "I'll show you how."

I watched carefully. "Dad, what if I don't make it?" I asked.

He always saved his counsel for when it counted most. "If you give it all you've got, you'll make it." As I stood watching those skeeters skim the surface of the water, Dad offered his next suggestion. "Honey, you have to keep your eye on the bank on the other side. It's keeping your eye on the target that makes all the difference."

I nodded. Then, taking a deep breath, I tightened my grip on the shovel, glanced quickly at Dad, gave it all I had, and swung forward. I made it safely to the other side of the ditch. Quickly I looked back at Dad; he was giving his usual sign for victory, clasping both hands together, raising them above his head, and shouting as though it were a glorious accomplishment, "I knew you could do it!"

I then watched as he jumped the ditch with such ease that I wondered why he'd made all that fuss for me. As a benediction to our morning ritual, Dad spoke in a tone that remains with me yet. "Ardie, my dear," he said, "there are a lot of irrigation ditches to cross in life. Many of them you must cross alone." Then, as a final summary to his lesson, he repeated, "Keep your eye on the other side and give it all you've got, and you will make it."

With a vision of the other side always in our minds and hearts, which vision is strengthened through our ordinances and covenants, we will make it all the way to the highest degree in the celestial kingdom (see D&C 131:1–2). And our Father will be there and will say to each of us in a loving and important way, "I knew you could do it."

I bear witness that it is through faithful obedience

to our covenants that we are sustained through the heat and the cold of life. As we drink of the living water that quenches spiritual thirst, our thirst can indeed be quenched. We will get that living water inside, and we will make it to the other side.

For it must needs be, that there is an opposition in all things. If not so, . . . righteousness could not be brought to pass.

—2 Nephi 2:11

10

PRAY FOR A STRONG BACK

There must be opposition if we are to develop strength.

I have come to understand that to honestly pray for a strong back is a very courageous thing to do. When we do so, we may be getting more than we had bargained for. The spiritual exercise required for such strengthening will not be easy, but the promised blessings will make it worth the cost, however high it may seem.

I first learned of the importance of a strong back when I was about ten years old. In the summer, after we had put in a full day's work, my father would take me down to the Belly River near the edge of our small town, Glenwood, which was not far from the Cardston

Alberta Temple. There he taught me to swim. But it wasn't simple swimming he wanted to teach. He taught me to eventually jump off the pier into the cold water and swim upstream against the current. It wasn't easy. It took a lot of courage and determination. As I recall, the water was always cold, and for me it seemed very swift. What made it possible was my father swimming along beside me, constantly encouraging me. I can hear his voice in my mind even today. "You can make it. Keep going."

By the end of the summer the water in the river had receded, and the swiftness of the current had subsided considerably—but only after I had learned the lesson: there must be opposition if we are to develop strength. The river had served the purpose my father had in mind. My back was stronger from the consistent effort.

Today we face tremendous opposition, and we must be prepared to swim against the current. We must be strong enough to take a stand and to defend our values. We must be courageous enough to speak up and speak out, to register our vote, to stand firm for truth and righteousness under all circumstances. We are swimming upstream against a river of opposition.

What a blessing to know that we will never be given more than we can handle with the Lord's help.

President Hinckley recently spoke of the challenges we face: "In the Church we are working very hard to stem the tide of [this] evil. But it is an uphill battle and we sometimes wonder whether we are making any headway. But we are succeeding in a substantial way. We must not give up. We must not become discouraged."[1]

STRENGTH THROUGH COVENANTS

When we pray for a strong back, we learn that it is through our covenants with the Lord that we are strengthened far beyond our natural ability. The testimony of President George Q. Cannon explains this relationship: "When we went into the waters of baptism and covenanted with our Father in heaven to serve Him and keep His commandments, He bound Himself also by covenant to us that He would never desert us, never leave us to ourselves, never forget us, that in the midst of trials and hardships, when everything was arrayed against us, He would be near unto us and would sustain us."[2]

Honoring our covenants is the way (and the only way) to swim against the escalating opposition of our day. When we are baptized and confirmed members of The Church of Jesus Christ of Latter-day Saints, we are given the gift of the Holy Ghost. We renew the covenant of baptism by partaking of the sacred emblems of the sacrament. Each week during the sacrament we have the blessing and opportunity to strengthen our backs and fill our spiritual reservoirs. We hear in our minds and hearts the words of the covenant to *always* remember him and keep his commandments so we can *always* have his Spirit to be with us (see D&C 20:77, 79). This should be our most earnest desire. Nothing will prepare us to stand against the opposing forces like the blessing and power of the gift of the Holy Ghost.

The Holy Ghost is a messenger who provides personal revelation, communication, and connection with our Father in Heaven and our Savior, Jesus Christ. We should do all within our power to keep the communication lines open. We can pledge to allow no compromise or justification that will separate us from the Lord; we can determine to make no excuse to tolerate any enticement of the world—in our entertainment or other activities—that will diminish the presence of the Spirit in our lives. Let us strive every day to avoid anything and everything that could weaken our spirits and extinguish the light. Let us simply give up our sins, turn our backs on them, and walk away.

Elder David B. Haight helped us understand the strength that can be found in our temple covenants, not only for our backs but for every fiber of our soul. He said, "A temple is a place in which those whom He has chosen [that's all of us] are endowed with power from on high—a power which enables us to use our gifts and capabilities with greater intelligence and increased effectiveness in order to bring to pass our Heavenly Father's purposes in our own lives and the lives of those we love."

He continued, "Come to the temples worthily and regularly. . . . Freely partake of the promised personal revelation that may bless your life with power, knowledge, light, beauty, and truth from on high, which will guide you and your posterity to eternal life."[3]

STRENGTH THROUGH TRIALS

In a very significant chapter in the Book of Mormon, Father Lehi explained to his son Jacob the need for opposition. "For it must needs be, that there is an opposition in all things. If not so, . . . righteousness could not be brought to pass" (2 Nephi 2:11). One of the primary purposes of this life is for us to be tried and tested in preparation to receive all the blessings the Lord has promised those who love him and keep his commandments (see D&C 136:31).

We can *expect* trials and tribulation—that is an essential part of the great plan. Some will come because of our own mistakes or sins, others are merely a part of living in mortality, and still others come because the Lord loves us and seeks to provide experiences that will increase our spiritual growth. "For whom the Lord loveth he chasteneth," Paul wrote (Hebrews 12:6). The chastening doesn't seem so hard once we understand its purpose. There are times when we must trust in the Lord with all our hearts, even when we don't understand (see Proverbs 3:5).

As Elder Bruce Hafen has taught: "If you have problems in your life, don't assume there is something wrong with you. Struggling with those problems is at the very core of life's purpose. As we draw close to God, He will show us our weaknesses and through them make us wiser, stronger."[4]

Some years ago Sister Jana Taylor, a faithful sister missionary who had committed to be totally obedient and strive to have the Spirit with her always, was having some very difficult, discouraging, and challenging times—not unlike a typical mission. If we are committed to really make a difference, the adversary seems to take notice and will often increase the swiftness of the current, increasing the opposition that would, if possible, carry us downstream, away from our goal. The day before Sister Taylor was to return home from her mission, she stood before her peers to bear testimony. She had a glow about her, a confidence different from when she arrived. "I'm thankful," she said, "for the challenges and the trials I've had. I'm thankful for every single hard day." She paused, then added, "And every day was hard. If it hadn't been, I wouldn't be who I am now. I am not the same person I was when I came out." And because of those hard times she will never be the same person again. She had, as the scripture says, begun to "grow up" in the Lord (see D&C 109:15). And her growing continues.

The writings of Orson F. Whitney help us understand the need for adversity: "No pain that we suffer, no trial that we experience is wasted. It ministers to our education, to the development of such qualities as patience, faith, fortitude, and humility. All that we suffer and all that we endure, especially when we endure it patiently, builds up our characters, purifies our hearts, expands our souls, and makes us more tender and charitable, more worthy to be called the children of

God. . . . And it is through sorrow and suffering, toil and tribulation, that we gain the education that we came here to acquire and which will make us more like our Father and Mother in heaven."[5]

While serving as matron of the Cardston Alberta Temple for three years, I witnessed many strong backs. I saw those stooped with age and those who traveled long distances to enter within the walls of the temple. But more significant than the physical distance of miles was the distance many traveled in terms of inward desire, refining their priorities and commitment.

One day a young woman, Annae Jensen, came to the temple to receive her endowment. I could feel the radiance of her spirit. This young woman was born without any arms—nothing beyond her shoulders. However, she seemed to have lost awareness of her physical limitation and had been spiritually compensated.

Just this past month, my husband and I received a call from Annae and Garath Jones (whom she had married) telling us of their blessing and excitement. They are expecting their first baby in just a few months—the beginning of their posterity. In my mind I saw this faithful young mother without arms and thought of her desire to cradle and love this special little spirit. I asked Annae, knowing she would respond positively, "How have you learned to handle the hard things in life?" In her usual happy, upbeat tone she said, "I just say, 'Heavenly Father, what am I supposed to learn from this?' And if I don't learn it, I've missed an opportunity."

While Annae is without arms, her back is strong. She has developed spirituality under what would appear to be adversity. There is no question—that baby will be encircled in its mother's love.

"I WILL . . . DELIVER THEM"

The Book of Mormon gives us many examples of how the Lord intervenes when we turn to him—and how trials and tribulation turn to our good. When Alma and his people were being persecuted by Amulon—the leader of the priests of the wicked King Noah—they began to pray mightily to God. In answer, the voice of the Lord came to the people of Alma, just as it will come to us. The Lord said, "I know of the covenant which ye have made unto me; and I will covenant with my people and deliver them out of bondage" (Mosiah 24:13).

From this story we learn some very significant lessons. The Lord told Alma's people he would ease the burdens on their backs, even to the extent that they wouldn't be able to feel them. But their complete deliverance from bondage would not happen all at once. To do so would not have allowed for the growth that took place as they learned to trust in him. The Lord explained this when he said, "This will I do that ye may stand as witnesses for me hereafter, and that ye may know of a surety that I, the Lord God, do visit my people in their afflictions" (Mosiah 24:14). Learning to carry the burden with ease allowed them to bear witness from personal experience that the Lord does watch over us in our adversities.

With the Lord's help, we can sometimes receive the same blessing in our own lives: "And now it came to pass that the burdens which were laid upon Alma and his brethren were made light; yea, the Lord did strengthen them that they could bear up their burdens with ease, and they did submit cheerfully and with patience to all the will of the Lord" (Mosiah 24:15).

And the lesson continues. Because of their great faith and patience through their trials, the Lord eventually spoke to them again. He would not only ease their burdens, he said, but as he had promised in the beginning, he would deliver them. "Be of good comfort, for on the morrow I will deliver you out of bondage" (Mosiah 24:16).

We know *about* our Savior—but it is often in our adversities that we truly find him and know him and love him. In our times of trial, if we turn to him, the Spirit bears witness that the Lord not only can but will ease our burdens. I can testify from my own experience that some of our heaviest burdens, disappointments, and heartaches can, in time, be replaced with the peace that passeth all understanding. The key is to wait upon the Lord through the trial.

In the words of Elder Neal A. Maxwell, "We can say; 'I know that [God] loveth his children; nevertheless, I do not know the meaning of all things' (1 Nephi 11:17). There have been and will be times in each of our lives when such faith must be the bottom line: We don't know what is happening to us or around us, but we know that God loves us, and knowing that, for the moment, is enough."[6]

Sisters, we each have a work to do. Our trials and tests are an important part of our preparation. The Lord is counting on us to stand firm, with strong backs, throughout each trial.

BURDENS OF OUR OWN MAKING

Now let us consider burdens that are of our own making. Some think that filling a daily planner with activities, events, and lists of good things to do helps to define them as successful. But the burden slowly grows heavier and heavier until, without noticing it, they are in danger of being swept downstream with osteoporosis.

President Kimball's statement about life invites some thoughtful contemplation. He said, "Since immortality and eternal life constitute the sole purpose of life, all other interests and activities are but incidental thereto."[7] Does that suggest there should be no time for fun, sports, scrapbooking, shopping, or fancy parties? Of course not! We can make time to do many worthwhile things, as long as they do not distract us from what matters most, the very purpose of life.

The feeling of being controlled by our schedules or the demands of others—or being out of control—is contrary to our divine nature. We cannot feel the Spirit or experience the peace and joy of each day when we are burdened beyond our ability to handle it all. I believe that if it were possible, the adversary would keep us busily engaged in a multitude of good things in an effort to keep us distracted from the few vital things that make all the difference. Deciding what we really want in life is a significant and powerful tool.

It gives us a sense of being in control of our lives, rather than being controlled.

The task of cutting back on some of our activities can be extremely challenging. It may seem as painful as cutting off an arm or a leg. It requires a sharp knife and determination. Pruning is hard. It usually comes only after pondering and praying to know what we're willing to cut out so we can provide more time for what we really desire. I love Michael McLean's song "Hold On, the Light Will Come." But as we look at our busy lives we might sing, "Let go of some things, so the light can come."

When we realize that our time is our life, we can begin to understand that whatever we do with our time is actually paid for with our life. What an awesome thought in today's world, where we are bombarded with so much with which we can fill every hour of every day. The Holy Ghost will guide us and help us know what to hang on to and what to let go of—and he will also help us pace ourselves as we face the arduous swim against the current.

The writings of Jacob teach us the need for pruning, cutting back, and thinning the branches. The lord of the vineyard looks at his dying trees and says to the dedicated servant the things we might say when we have concerns for the welfare of our family. "But what could I have done more in my vineyard? Have I slackened my hand, that I have not nourished it? Nay, I have nourished it, and I have digged about it . . . ; and I have stretched forth mine hand almost all the day long. . . . What could I have done more?" (Jacob 5:47, 49). Sound familiar?

The servant then explains the problem. The vineyard didn't go bad because of a lack of dedication or hard work on the part of the lord of the vineyard. The branches of the tree—like our overcrowded lives— had overcome the roots by growing faster than the roots, taking the strength unto themselves and leaving the roots undernourished (see Jacob 5:48).

The first responsibility to ease the burden on our backs rests with us. We must take time to *ponder,* to *pray,* and to *prune.* Perhaps it would be a good idea to ponder the question that Nephi was asked when he was swept away by the Spirit. When the Spirit said to him, "What desirest thou?" Nephi was prepared with an answer (see 1 Nephi 11:2–3). If we were asked "What desirest thou?" when we go to the Lord in prayer, would we be ready with an answer? Do we know what we really want? More important, do we know what we want to have happen, and why?

I can hear one of my darling nieces say something like, "What I most desire is to make it through the whole day without being impatient or raising my voice. Or just to catch my breath for a few moments before the troops come home. Or just to feel loved, appreciated, and in control." Certainly all that is reasonable and real, but when time is provided to get an eternal perspective and see beyond the urgencies of the day, our perspective changes. We are willing, even anxious, to do some pruning, some cutting back, if that would provide more time for the things we most desire. In the process, we will eliminate some of the burdens of our own making.

COURAGEOUS WOMEN WITH STRONG BACKS

I have been impressed with the moving account of Emma Smith's most earnest desires at a very challenging time in her life. When her husband decided to return to Carthage—a fateful decision that would lead to his death—she asked him to give her a blessing. Joseph asked her to "write down the best blessing she desired and he would sign it upon his return." That tells us something about the confidence the Prophet had in the desires of Emma's heart. He never returned from Carthage. But we have a record of her desires at that fateful time in her life. She wrote ten things she most desired. The first sentence began, "I crave," and the following nine, "I desire." I would like to share with you her first and last statements.

"First of all that I would crave, as the richest of heaven's blessings, would be wisdom from my Heavenly Father bestowed daily, so that whatever I might do or say, I could not look back at the close of day with regret, or neglect the performance of any act that would bring a blessing." She completed her list with this statement, "Finally I desire that whatever may be my lot through life I may be enabled to acknowledge the hand of God in all things."[8] Under the most severe testing during that crucial time in the history of the Church, Emma Smith's desires tell us something of the strength of her back.

There are courageous women among us today and those who will follow after us when we do our part. In the poetic words of Mormon pioneer Vilate Raile, we see this legacy of faith passed from one generation to the next.

> They cut desire into short lengths
> And fed it to the hungry fires of courage.
> Long after, when the flames had died,
> Molten Gold gleamed in the ashes.

> *They gathered it into bruised palms*
> *And handed it to their children*
> *And their children's children*
> *Forever.*[9]

Sisters, we are on the Lord's errand. We can have his Spirit to be with us always, with angels round about us to bear us up. My great-grandmother Susan Kent Greene is one who understood this, and she understood something about strong backs. In 1835, Susan married Evan M. Greene and soon after went to Kirtland to live. They were among the first of the Mormon fugitives at Mount Pisgah, Iowa, in the early spring of 1846. We read, "As soon as Evan pitched the tent he left his wife and their little ones while he went with his team and wagon to aid in bringing forward some of the saints who were without means of their own. Unfortunately for Susan she had no near neighbors. Almost as soon as her husband had gone the eleven-month old baby became ill. The baby rapidly grew worse, and after a few days died in its mother's arms. This occurred on a dark and stormy night accompanied by loud thunderbolts and vivid lightning flashes. All she could do was to pray that the Lord would not forsake her, but would send someone to help her, which prayer was answered. A young man came to the door and spoke words of pity and comfort. In the morning he made a coffin and dug a grave for the baby and buried it. Susan had to prepare the little body for its last rest, herself."[10]

This was only the beginning of the tests that were to follow.

Evan and Susan arrived in Utah, having endured much. She wrote on the first page of her journal, dated February 3, 1875: "I make this covenant to do the very best I can asking God for wisdom to direct me in that I may walk with him in all righteousness and truth. I much desire to be pure in heart that I may see God. Help me Lord to overcome all evil with good. This covenant with the writings on this page is written with my blood and I have not broken my covenant and trust I shall not. Signed, Susan K. Greene."[11]

I look forward to one day meeting my great-grandmother. I pray that I can tell her that I have followed her path, having myself kept the faith and all the covenants.

With an understanding of the purpose of life, the need for opposition, and our promised blessings as women of the covenant, let us be grateful that God allows us to struggle, to cry, and to feel pain. How else could we comfort others in their tribulation? (see 2 Corinthians 1:6).

Let us be grateful that we can know about hurt and healing. How else could we know the Healer, the Great Physician, who invites us to come unto Him and be healed? (see D&C 42:48).

Let us be grateful to know about fear and faith. How else would we recognize the light of faith after the dark night of fear? (see D&C 6:36).

Let us be grateful to know about discouragement and encouragement. How else could we reach out and take another's hand in empathy, understanding, and love? (see John 13:34).

Let us be grateful to know about offenses and forgiveness. How else how could we ever begin to appreciate the atonement? (see Alma 7:11).

Let us be grateful for His infinite love, and let us hear in our minds and hearts His words of comfort: "What I say unto one I say unto all, be of good cheer, little children; for I am in your midst, and I have not forsaken you" (D&C 61:36).

I testify that in difficult times, when our crosses seem unbearable, he who carried the cross for all of us—our Lord and Savior, Jesus Christ—will sustain us, be with us, and will be the strength in our backs as we turn to him in earnest, fervent, sincere, and humble prayer.

That which is of God is light; and he that receiveth light,
and continueth in God, receiveth more light; and that
light groweth brighter and brighter until the perfect day.
—Doctrine and Covenants 50:24

ARISE AND SHINE
FORTH

IT IS THROUGH THE COVENANTS MADE IN THE
TEMPLE THAT WE FIND OUR GREATEST SOURCE OF
LIGHT AND KNOWLEDGE AND POWER.

I had gone to Tucson, Arizona, to spend a few wonderful and memorable days with my niece, Shelly, as she gave birth to her fourth little boy. Prior to the delivery, three young boys waited anxiously for the arrival of their little brother, who was making the transition from his heavenly home to his experience on earth. Now he had joined them, and each little brother took turns reverently cradling this tiny baby in their arms. It seemed as if they already knew him.

Soon after this moment of reverence and celebration, I was sitting at the kitchen table with these young children painting rocks, making birds and fish and bugs and other creative possibilities. Six-year-old Josh, holding his paintbrush and looking very serious, asked the question, "How many birthdays do you have left, Nana Ardie?"

I smiled and asked, "What do you mean, Josh?"

He reached out his arms to give me a hug and said, "I love you, and I don't want you to ever die."

I wrapped him in my arms and felt a tender bond with this precious child. At that moment the reality of mortality and immortality swept through my mind; I saw it as a glorious drama in which we all take part. We enter this life as a baby, and then, in what seems like so few birthdays, there comes a time for us to return. We each have our time on stage.

With my arm around this little blond-headed boy, realizing that Easter was upon us, I said, "Josh, I have something wonderful to tell you. I don't know how many birthdays I have left, but that part doesn't really matter. What really matters is to know that Jesus came to this earth like your little baby brother. He did what he came to do; then he died and was resurrected. Because of his great love for everyone, he made it possible that there would never be an end to our love for each other. When I say good-bye to you and go back words for our day: "Let us therefore cast off the works of darkness, and let us put on the armour of light" (Romans 13:12). The "armour of light" is a shield against darkness, and with that shield we will have the courage to respond to the Lord's call. The words of the Prophet Joseph Smith during the severe tests of the Nauvoo period speak of courage: "Shall we not go on in so great a cause? Go forward and not backward. Courage . . . ; and on, on to the victory!" (D&C 128:22).

Don't you just want to enlist, sign up, suit up in the armor of light and be part of this royal army "with banner, sword, and shield," with a sure knowledge that there will be "victory, victory, thru Jesus Christ, our Lord"?[3]

The world is in chaos, and we are called to make a difference, to arise and shine here and now in our nation, our town, our community, our neighborhood, the street in which we live or where we may be called to serve. Make no mistake, you and I have a vital part to play in this second estate. It is our second act, so to speak. And believe me, it will take courage. We may feel inadequate, unprepared, unworthy, or fearful, but that is no excuse. Many, many others have felt the same way. With God's help the light of Christ will

to Utah, we still keep loving each other and look forward to seeing each other again. In the same way, when I run out of birthdays I will go back home, but we will still keep loving each other and look forward to when we will be together again."

He smiled and went back to painting his rock, and into my mind came the words of Helaman to his sons: "And now, my sons, remember, remember that it is upon the rock of our Redeemer, who is Christ, the Son of God, that ye must build your foundation; that when the devil shall send forth his mighty winds, yea, his shafts in the whirlwind, yea, when all his hail and his mighty storm shall beat upon you, it shall have no power over you to drag you down to the gulf of misery and endless wo, because of the rock upon which ye are built, which is a sure foundation, a foundation whereon if men build they cannot fall" (Helaman 5:12). It is an assurance of Christ's atonement that eases the concern for how many birthdays we have left.

Yes, the mighty winds will blow. There will be times when we may feel caught in a whirlwind. The hailstorms in our lives can leave us feeling rushed and pushed and out of control, with a sense that we should be accomplishing more, that we should be better than we are. It is at these times that we can listen to the voice within, speaking words of peace, "You're better than you think you are." Consider the Christmas message of the First Presidency—President Hinckley, President Monson, and President Faust—on December 7, 2003, when they reminded us, "The Prince of Peace, who stilled the tempest on the Sea of Galilee, has the power to calm the storms in our personal lives."[1]

THIS IS OUR TIME

I couldn't tell Josh how many birthdays I have left. I don't know. But I do know that it is possible to find joy and happiness and peace of mind in every day. Our Savior made it possible. Like my four little nephews, we each left our heavenly home at this specific time to come to earth for an uncertain number of birthdays. This is our time, sisters, and what a time it is! Prophets from all previous dispensations have anxiously anticipated the glorious day in which we now live. Some starry night, go out alone and in wonderment look up at the endless sky and ponder deep within you the questions, Why me? Why now? Why here?

President Gordon B. Hinckley's words on the eve of the twenty-first century speak of our time and our

responsibility: "May God bless us with a sense of place in history, and having been given that sense, a need to stand tall and walk with resolution in a ner becoming the Saints of the most high."[2]

In the early history of the Church, a revelat given through the Prophet Joseph Smith at for all members of the Church "scattered ab the world" (D&C 115:3). That revelation i from the Lord for our day: "Verily I say Arise and shine forth, that thy light may for the nations" (D&C 115:5).

Do we read this only as a line from t tory? Do we view it as a simple i involved? Or do we hear it as an u hearts and in our minds? It is a call tual strength sufficient to raise the same fervor Captain Moroni ha "rent his coat; . . . and wrote up our God, our religion, and freed wives, and our children" (Al same values burning within o raising the standard, whatev no mistake, we each have a able season.

The Apostle Paul, in s

shine through us. The war that was begun in heaven is raging here upon the earth, and we, once again, must take sides for or against the kingdom of God. With the assurance that we performed well in the first act, let us go forth with confidence, optimism, and, yes, anticipation as faithful Latter-day Saints, each doing our part as we come to realize our foreordained roles in this great drama in human history. What a tremendous time for us to be on stage.

MOLDING AND SHAPING

King Benjamin explains the challenge we face as mortals here on earth: "For the natural man is an enemy to God," and so we will remain until we yield "to the enticings of the Holy Spirit, and [put] off the natural man and [become] a saint through the atonement of Christ the Lord." As part of that process, we will become "submissive, . . . willing to submit to all things which the Lord seeth fit to inflict upon [us], even as a child doth submit to his father" (Mosiah 3:19).

When we willingly submit to the will of our Father in Heaven and strive to follow the promptings we receive though the Spirit, we can expect some molding and shaping, some refining and cutting away. This can be difficult and, yes, painful.

The story is told of a great sculptor who worked hour after hour in his studio carving, chipping, shaping, relentlessly cutting away day after day. He seemed to be driven by a sense of mission. A young girl often came by to watch. One day during the process her eyes lit up as she exclaimed, "I know who that is. That is Abraham Lincoln. How did you know he was in there?"

Our Father in Heaven knows us, knows what we have the capacity to become and has a plan for us. When we willingly submit to the molding and shaping and to some intense chipping away, we will discover our divine destiny: who and whose we really are. The Prophet Joseph Smith, in describing his life of trials and tests, said, "I am like a huge, rough stone rolling down from a high mountain, and the only polishing I get is when some corner gets rubbed off by coming in contact with something else, striking with accelerated force ... knocking off a corner here and a corner there. Thus I would become a smooth and polished shaft in the quiver of the Almighty."[4]

Our Father in Heaven has a plan to ensure our eternal happiness if we choose to follow. And because he loves us, he will smooth and polish us with trials and tests, not to destroy us but to sanctify us. Responding to the call to rise and shine, we must seek the light in earnest daily prayer. There is great power in prayer. We will be receptive to the promptings of the Holy Spirit by keeping the commandments. President Benson explained, "When obedience ceases to be an irritant and becomes our quest, in that moment God will endow us with power."[5]

We will be guided day by day in our foreordained mission. President George Q. Cannon wrote: "God has chosen us out of the world and has given us a great mission. We were selected and foreordained for this mission before the world was. . . . We had our parts allotted to us in this mortal state of existence as our Savior had his assigned to him."[6]

Does your responsibility seem overwhelming at times, or does it awaken within you a realization, perhaps a memory, of who you really are and your capacity to make a difference in such a way that your light will literally be a standard in your area of influence? Clearly Satan desires to have us (see 3 Nephi 18:18), and he wants to reinforce any feelings of inadequacy we may have. He seeks to diminish our light, our righteous influence. We hesitate sometimes to open our mouths, not because we are ashamed of the gospel of Jesus Christ, but perhaps because we sense a lack of ability to explain what we feel in our hearts. It has been said, "It takes courage to take a stand when values are compromised for convenience and popularity is preferred over principle."[7] But stand we must, even if it requires standing alone.

I'm impressed by the words of Joan of Arc in the play *Joan of Lorraine* by Maxwell Anderson. She says, "I know this now: every man gives his life for what he believes. Every woman gives her life for what she believes. Sometimes people believe in little or nothing. One life is all we have. We live it as we believe in living it and then it's gone. But to surrender what you are and live without belief, that's more terrible than dying, more terrible than dying young."[8]

"I WILL COME IN TO HIM"

The question, of course, is not what we are willing to die for but rather what we are willing to live for. Sometimes the journey is difficult, very difficult, but the Lord has promised the light will come. "Behold, I stand at the door, and knock: if any man hear my voice, and open the door, I will come in to him, and will sup with him, and he with me" (Revelation 3:20).

Could it ever be that he would knock and we would not open the door? Perhaps we cannot hear the knock because the voices of despair, discouragement, and disappointment drown out the whisperings of the Spirit.

I vividly remember a very difficult time in my own life many years ago. It was Thanksgiving Day. The image of Thanksgiving in my mind pictured large, happy families everywhere gathered around bounteous tables with children and grandchildren, parents and grandparents, and joy inexpressible, the future bright. With the reality of only two plates on our Thanksgiving table, no family near, and no children, the room seemed dark. The light was fading rapidly.

I learned on that occasion, and many others since then, that when we invite him in to sup with us, we need never be alone. Our tables are laden, and the room is filled with light. And then like a "letter from home" we hear in our minds and hearts the promise, "And if your eye be single to my glory, your whole bodies shall be filled with light, and there shall be no darkness in you; and that body which is filled with light comprehendeth all things" (D&C 88:67). We begin to see things differently; we see the hand of the Lord in our lives; we learn to trust in the Lord with all our hearts and not lean on our own understanding (see

Proverbs 3:5). Then we can help light the way for others.

"THE LIGHT GROWETH BRIGHTER"

I've been speaking about light. There are two kinds of light. There is a physical light by which we see, which can affect our moods and have a great impact on our physical health. We know something of the clinical use of light, as in light therapy. But there is a greater light, which is not subject to sunrise, sunset, or any weather condition. It is not subject to disappointment, despair, or distress. This light can penetrate the darkest days and the heaviest storm clouds in every season. This is the spiritual light that is available to each of us. We read in the Doctrine and Covenants, "That which is of God is light; and he that receiveth light, and continueth in God, receiveth more light; and that light groweth brighter and brighter until the perfect day" (D&C 50:24). We know that "whatsoever is light is Spirit, even the Spirit of Jesus Christ" (D&C 84:45).

When you and I went into the waters of baptism, we covenanted to keep the commandments and to stand as a witness for Christ at all times so we can always have his Spirit to be with us. We cannot be a brilliant light, or even a modest light, by ourselves. We need help. And help is always available.

RESISTING EVIL

I'm impressed with the words of President George Q. Cannon concerning any confrontation with evil: "When Satan comes and assails us it is our privilege to say, 'Get thee behind me, Satan, for I have no lot nor portion in you and you have no part in me. I'm in the service of God and I'm going to serve him. And you can do what you please, it is no use your presenting yourself with your blandishments to me. . . . I will not listen to you. I will close my heart against you.'"[9]

We are placed here as moral agents to develop our divine nature. "If we were not surrounded by darkness," explained President Cannon, "we could not develop. Good and evil must be presented before us. We are free to do right or to do wrong and to choose the path we shall tread."[10]

We choose what we expose our faculties to by way of sights, sounds, thoughts, and feelings. The consequences of our choices are fixed, and when we choose the right we hunger and thirst after righteousness. But if the conduit for the Spirit becomes polluted by what we choose to expose our minds to and the light goes out, the hunger and thirst for the things of the world can become an enslaving addiction. Can we be casual about what we expose our minds to?

King Benjamin, in one of his last, great addresses, warned: "I cannot tell you all the things whereby ye may commit sin; for there are divers ways and means, even so many that I cannot number them. But this much I can tell you, that if ye do not watch yourselves, and your thoughts, and your words, and your deeds, and observe the commandments of God, and continue in the faith of what ye have heard concerning the coming of our Lord, even unto the end of your lives, ye must perish" (Mosiah 4:29–30).

The light will dim and we'll gradually die out. It has been said, "In the armory of thought, [man] forges the weapons by which he destroys himself."[11]

THE LIGHT OF THE TEMPLE

The growth of God's kingdom in these latter days is commensurate with the faithful followers of Christ who hold the line. Every effort to seek the light, follow the light, be the light, and share the light will shine through every act of service, every truth taught, every commandment obeyed, every resistance to evil, every effort to share the gospel, and every prayer. When no one is watching our performance and there is no public applause, in the still, quiet moments we will feel our Heavenly Father's approval. With a sincere desire and commitment to arise and shine forth, that our light may be a standard for the nations, we will be drawn to the light that comes through the ordinances and covenants of the temple. President Packer reminds us: "In the temple, we face the sunlight of truth. The light of the temple, that understanding, shines upon us as does the light of the sun. And the shadows of sin and ignorance and error, of disappointment and failure, fall behind us. Nowhere quite equals the temple."[12]

Brother Kapp and I have had the opportunity to spend much time in the temple. I have had my eyes opened and my understanding increased as never before. I have a deeper sense of the magnitude and the vastness and eternal nature of ordinances and covenants available in the temple. It is through the covenants made in the temple that we find our greatest source of light and knowledge and power. It is in the ordinances of the temple that we begin to more fully comprehend the very purpose of this earthly journey and the great plan of happiness. We learn of our divine inheritance as a child of God and our potential as an eternal being. In the temple we learn to see things differently. Our values change. The light of the temple helps us gain an eternal perspective. Our covenant relationship with the Savior strengthens our desire and our commitment to arise and shine forth. We know that with his help we can do better than we've ever done before. The temple helps us to see that we're better than we think we are.

The grandest blessing of the temple is the sealing power that unites families. It has been said, "The marriage relationship, more than any other, because it is more intimate, more constant, more important, is our greatest spiritual challenge and has the greatest potential, along with parenthood, to make us godlike."

Successful marriage partners find it more effective to use a challenging experience to tutor themselves, rather than to coach their spouses. The challenge is not to train our companion but to train ourselves to focus on what is right rather than what is wrong, to be intent on fixing the relationship rather than fixing the blame. Satan is real. His influence is real. The battle is raging and evil influences are marshaled to create contention, conflict, misunderstanding, and miscommunication and to use every effort to weaken the husband and wife relationship and destroy families. If that happens, the enemy scores a victory and he laughs.

In the temple we learn more of the great plan of happiness and our reasons for unwavering hope. We learn of the promises in relation to our covenants, and we feel God's binding love. When I was serving as matron in the Cardston Alberta Temple, the Primary theme one year was "I Love to See the Temple; I'm Going There Someday." During that year I had the opportunity to speak to many, many children in small groups and to learn from them. Each time I saw a command performance of those willing to arise and shine. There is a light that emanates from such a gathering.

Addressing one group of children, I asked, "How are you preparing to come to the temple?" Their arms shot straight in the air, eager to tell. One child on the front row, his arm straight in the air, exploded with his wisdom, "Be good." Another gave additional wisdom: "Don't eat bad stuff." And another: "Do what is right, no matter what." (I was told that one child, when asked if his whole family kept the Word of Wisdom, responded regretfully, "All but Grandpa. He puts tobacco sauce on his food.")

Then I asked, "How many of you are preparing and looking forward to coming to the temple and being married in the temple?" Every hand went up. I asked them, "How many of you are trying to be obedient?" Once again I received a unanimous response. One more question: "What do you do to be obedient?" A quick answer, "Do what your mom says." Is it any wonder that we are to become even as a child, as the scripture teaches us? (see Mosiah 3:19).

"Shine for Him Each Day"

As a child in Primary, I remember standing and singing with my whole heart and soul, "Jesus wants me for a sunbeam, to shine for him each day."[13] I remember feeling like he really needed me, and I remember how I felt deep inside singing, "I'll be a sunbeam for him." He still needs us, sisters, to shine for him each day. We can do it if we but try. He will magnify our efforts.

We may never carry the light, the flame, the fire of the Olympic torch with the world looking on, but we can be a bright and burning flame as we pass the cleansing light of Christ to every nation, through every generation. Let us do our part with the same conviction and enthusiasm as those children at the temple.

The light from the temple is passed from one generation to the next through those who arise and shine forth to take a stand and make a commitment to endure whatever difficulty or hardship is required. May it be recorded for generations to come that during our brief time of trial and test in this earth-life experience, we did arise and shine forth fearlessly, courageously, and boldly. President Hinckley, in a voice of warning for our day, tells us: "You cannot simply take for granted this cause, which is the cause of Christ. You cannot simply stand on the sidelines and watch the play between the forces of good and evil. Said Nephi, 'They who are not for me are against me, saith our God' (2 Nephi 10:16)."[14]

While we do not know how many birthdays we have left, we do know that while we are here we can experience and accomplish remarkable things. I am impressed with the words of Rachel Naomi Remen: "Days pass and the years vanish and we walk sightless among miracles. Lord, fill our eyes with seeing and our mind with knowing. Let there be moments when your Presence, like lightning, illuminates the darkness in which we walk. Help us to see wherever we gaze that the bush burns unconsumed and we, clay touched by God, will reach out for holiness and exclaim and wonder, how filled with awe is this place and we did not know it."[15]

When we are committed to give all we have with

faith in the Lord Jesus Christ, his light will shine through us, and we will be filled with awe at our opportunities to influence and to lift others. I bear witness, from a lifetime of experience, that God lives. He is our father; we are his children. Jesus Christ is our Savior and our Redeemer, the life and the light of the world. I pray that we will each resolve with increased determination to answer the call to arise and shine forth, that our light may be a standard for the nations. With the help of God we can shine as he would have us shine. We can be better than we think we are.

NOTES

Chapter 1: We Are Not Alone

1. Harold B. Lee, "Understanding Who We Are Brings Self-Respect," *Ensign*, January 1974, 7.
2. Gordon B. Hinckley, "The True Strength of the Church," *Ensign*, July 1973, 49.
3. James E. Faust, "A Personal Relationship with the Savior," *Ensign*, November 1976, 59.

Chapter 2: Better Than You Think You Are

1. Neal A. Maxwell, "Notwithstanding My Weakness," *Ensign*, November 1976, 12.
2. Joseph Smith, *Teachings of the Prophet Joseph Smith*, ed. Joseph Fielding Smith (Salt Lake City: Deseret Book, 1976), 348.
3. Joseph F. Smith, in *Journal of Discourses*, 26 vols. (Liverpool: Latter-day Saints' Book Depot, 1854–86), 24:78.
4. Gordon B. Hinckley, "Standing Strong and Immovable," Worldwide Leadership Training Meeting, January 10, 2004.
5. George Q. Cannon, *Gospel Truth: Discourses and Writings of President George Q. Cannon*, ed. Jerreld L. Newquist, 2 vols. (Salt Lake City: Deseret Book, 1987), 1:7.
6. Charles H. Gabriel, "I Stand All Amazed," *Hymns of The*

Church of Jesus Christ of Latter-day Saints (Salt Lake City: The Church of Jesus Christ of Latter-day Saints, 1985), no. 193.

7. Joy Saunders Lundberg, "I Am of Infinite Worth," in *I Walk By Faith* (Provo, Utah: Prime Recordings, 1986); used by permission.

8. Maxwell, "Notwithstanding My Weakness," 12.

9. Richard G. Scott, "Finding Forgiveness," *Ensign*, May 1995, 75.

10. Brigham Young, in *Journal of Discourses*, 4:268.

Chapter 3: Doubt Not, Fear Not

1. See Patricia T. Holland, "Within Whispering Distance of Heaven," in *Woman to Woman: Selected Talks from the BYU Women's Conferences* (Salt Lake City: Deseret Book, 1986), 115.

2. Dan Greenburg, with Marcia Jacobs, *How to Make Yourself Miserable: Another Vital Training Manual* (New York: Random House, 1966).

3. George Q. Cannon, *Gospel Truth: Discourses and Writings of President George Q. Cannon*, ed. Jerreld L. Newquist, 2 vols. (Salt Lake City: Deseret Book, 1987), 1:2.

4. Ezra Taft Benson, "Jesus Christ: Our Savior and Redeemer," *Ensign*, November 1983, 8.

5. Emily Dickinson, "We Never Know How High We Are," in *The Complete Poems of Emily Dickinson* (Boston: Little, Brown, and Company, 1924), Part One, Poem no. 97.

6. Eliza R. Snow, "How Great the Wisdom and the Love," *Hymns of The Church of Jesus Christ of Latter-day Saints* (Salt Lake City: The Church of Jesus Christ of Latter-day Saints, 1985), no. 195.

7. Charles H. Gabriel, "I Stand All Amazed," *Hymns*, no. 193.

8. James Montgomery, "Prayer Is the Soul's Sincere Desire," *Hymns*, no. 145.

9. Joseph Smith, *Teachings of the Prophet Joseph Smith*, ed. Joseph Fielding Smith (Salt Lake City: Deseret Book, 1976), 255.

10. Michael McLean, "She Doesn't Know," from *Safe Harbors* (Salt Lake City: Shadow Mountain, 1999); used by permission.

11. Cannon, *Gospel Truth*, 1:22.

Chapter 4: Away at School

1. Author unknown.

2. Bruce C. Hafen, *The Broken Heart: Applying the Atonement to Life's Experiences* (Salt Lake City: Deseret Book, 1989), 5–6.

3. LDS Bible Dictionary, "Prayer," 753.

4. Parley P. Pratt, *Key to the Science of Theology* (Salt Lake City: Deseret Book Company, 1965), 101.

5. Brigham Young, *Discourses of Brigham Young*, ed. John A. Widtsoe (Salt Lake City: Deseret Book, 1954), 43.

6. Dallin H. Oaks, "Revelation," in *BYU Speeches* (Provo, Utah: University Publications, 1982), 26.

7. Brigham Young, in *Journal of Discourses*, 26 vols. (Liverpool: Latter-day Saints' Book Depot, 1854–86), 6:94.

8. George Q. Cannon, *Gospel Truth: Discourses and Writings of President George Q. Cannon*, ed. Jerreld L. Newquist, 2 vols. (Salt Lake City: Deseret Book, 1987), 1:3.

Chapter 5: Cherish the Time

1. Thornton Wilder, *Our Town* (New York: Harper and Row, 1957), 100.

Chapter 6: You Can Make It

1. George Q. Cannon, *Gospel Truth: Discourses and Writings of President George Q. Cannon*, ed. Jerreld L. Newquist, 2 vols. (Salt Lake City: Deseret Book, 1987), 1:8.

Chapter 7: Miracle of Miracles

1. Sheldon Harnick, "Miracle of Miracles," in Jerry Bock, *Fiddler on the Roof* (New York: Pocket Books, 1966).
2. George Q. Cannon, *Gospel Truth: Discourses and Writings of President George Q. Cannon*, ed. Jerreld L. Newquist, 2 vols. (Salt Lake City: Deseret Book, 1987), 1:1.
3. *Teachings of Presidents of the Church: Heber J. Grant* (Salt Lake City: The Church of Jesus Christ of Latter-day Saints, 2003), 33.
4. W. H. Murray, *The Scottish Himalayan Expedition* (London: J. M. Dent & Sons, 1951).
5. As quoted by Andrea Ludlow Christensen, *BYU Magazine* (Summer 2004): 8.
6. Jill Mulvay Derr, Audrey M. Godfrey, and Kenneth W. Godfrey, *Women's Voices* (Salt Lake City: Deseret Book, 1982), 290.
7. Ardeth G. Kapp, *Miracles in Pinafores and Blue Jeans* (Salt Lake City: Deseret Book, 1977).
8. Ralph Waldo Emerson, "Self Reliance," in *American Literary Essays*, ed. Lewis Gaston Leary (New York: Crowell, 1960), 283, 284, 286.

Chapter 8: Where Do I Find My Strength?

1. William Ernest Henley, "Invictus," in Roy Jay Cook, *101 Famous Poems* (New York: Reilly & Lee, 1958), 95.

2. Neal A. Maxwell, *Meek and Lowly* (Salt Lake City: Deseret Book, 1987), 9.

3. Philip Paul Bliss, "More Holiness Give Me," *Hymns of The Church of Jesus Christ of Latter-day Saints* (Salt Lake City: The Church of Jesus Christ of Latter-day Saints, 1985), no. 131.

4. See LDS Bible Dictionary, "Grace," 697.

5. William Henry Monk, *Hymns Ancient and Modern* (New York: Pott, Young, and Company, 1874).

6. George Q. Cannon, *Gospel Truth: Discourses and Writings of President George Q. Cannon*, ed. Jerreld L. Newquist, 2 vols. (Salt Lake City: Deseret Book, 1987), 1:134.

7. Virginia H. Pearce, in *The Best of Women's Conference* (Salt Lake City: Deseret Book, 2000), 433.

Chapter 9: Never Thirst Again

1. John A. Widtsoe, in Conference Report, April 1952, 33–34.

2. *Deseret News*, Saturday, June 8, 1996.

3. Quoted by Harold B. Lee, in Conference Report, October 1955, 56.

4. William Fowler, "We Thank Thee, O God, for a Prophet," *Hymns of The Church of Jesus Christ of Latter-day Saints* (Salt Lake City: The Church of Jesus Christ of Latter-day Saints, 1985), no. 19.

5. Eliza R. Snow, "The Time Is Far Spent," *Hymns*, no. 266.

6. See Andrew F. Ehat and Lyndon W. Cook, *Words of Joseph Smith: The Contemporary Accounts of the Nauvoo Discourses of the Prophet Joseph* (Salt Lake City: Bookcraft, 1980), 157.

7. Tad Callister, *The Infinite Atonement* (Salt Lake City: Deseret Book, 2000), 296.

8. Elizabeth Barrett Browning, *Aurora Leigh*, book 7.

9. Brigham Young, *Discourses of Brigham Young*, ed. John A. Widtsoe (Salt Lake City: Deseret Book, 1954), 416.

10. See Ardeth G. Kapp, *The Temple, Our Home Away from Home* (Salt Lake City: Deseret Book, 2003), 1–15.

11. Ezra Taft Benson, *Teachings of Ezra Taft Benson* (Salt Lake City: Bookcraft, 1988), 256.

12. In *Glimpses into the Life and Heart of Marjorie Pay Hinckley*, ed. Virginia H. Pearce (Salt Lake City: Deseret Book, 1999), 193, 195.

Chapter 10: Pray for a Strong Back

1. Gordon B. Hinckley, "Standing Strong and Immovable," Worldwide Leadership Training Meeting, January 10, 2004, 20.

2. George Q. Cannon, *Gospel Truth: Discourses and Writings of President George Q. Cannon*, ed. Jerreld L. Newquist, 2 vols. (Salt Lake City: Deseret Book, 1987), 1:170.

3. David B. Haight, "Come to the House of the Lord," *Ensign*, May 1992, 15–16.

4. Bruce C. Hafen, "The Atonement: All for All," *Ensign*, May 2004, 97.

5. Orson F. Whitney, as quoted by Spencer W. Kimball, *Faith Precedes the Miracle* (Salt Lake City: Deseret Book, 1972), 98.

6. Neal A. Maxwell, *Not My Will, But Thine* (Salt Lake City: Deseret Book, 1988), 119.

7. Spencer W. Kimball, *Miracle of Forgiveness* (Salt Lake City: Bookcraft, 1969), 2.

8. Relief Society Course of Study, 1985 (Salt Lake City: The Church of Jesus Christ of Latter-day Saints, 1984), 199.

9. Cited in Asahel D. Woodruff, *Parent and Youth* (Salt Lake City: Deseret Sunday School Union Board, 1971), 124.

10. *Life Sketch of Susan Kent Greene by her daughter Louisa (Lula) Greene Richards.* In possession of author.

11. Ibid.

Chapter 11: Arise and Shine Forth

1. "First Presidency Christmas Message," *Liahona*, December 2003, 1.

2. Gordon B. Hinckley, "At the Summit of the Ages," *Ensign*, November 1999, 74.

3. Fanny J. Crosby, "Behold! A Royal Army," *Hymns of The Church of Jesus Christ of Latter-day Saints* (Salt Lake City: The Church of Jesus Christ of Latter-day Saints, 1985), no. 251.

4. Joseph Smith, *Teachings of the Prophet Joseph Smith*, ed. Joseph Fielding Smith (Salt Lake City: Deseret Book, 1976), 304.

5. Ezra Taft Benson, as quoted by Donald L. Staheli, in "Obedience, Life's Great Challenge," *Ensign*, May 1998, 81.

6. George Q. Cannon, *Gospel Truth: Discourses and Writings of President George Q. Cannon*, ed. Jerreld L. Newquist, 2 vols. (Salt Lake City: Deseret Book, 1987), 1:18.

7. Quoted in Ardeth G. Kapp, "Our Time Is Now," Brigham Young University–Idaho Educational Week Devotional, June 26, 2003.

8. Maxwell Anderson, *Joan of Lorraine* (Washington, D.C.: Anderson House, 1947).

9. Cannon, *Gospel Truth*, 1:17.

10. Ibid., 13.

11. James Allen, *As a Man Thinketh* (Salt Lake City: Bookcraft, 1964), 5.

12. Boyd K. Packer, *The Holy Temple* (Salt Lake City: Bookcraft, 1980), 42.

13. Nellie Talbot, "Jesus Wants Me for a Sunbeam," *Children's Songbook* (Salt Lake City: The Church of Jesus Christ of Latter-day Saints, 1989), 60.

14. Gordon B. Hinckley, "Stand Up for Truth," *BYU Speeches* (Provo, Utah: University Publications, 1997), 25.

15. Rachel Naomi Remen, *My Grandfather's Blessings* (New York: Riverhead Books, 2000), 72–73.

INDEX

Index